CAREER POWER

Unlock the Potential to Manage your own Future

CAREER POWER

Unlock the Potential to Manage your own Future

HILTON CATT AND PATRICIA SCUDAMORE

WARD LOCK

A WARD LOCK BOOK

First published in the UK 1997 by
Ward Lock
Wellington House
125 Strand, London WC2R 0BB

A Cassell Imprint

Copyright © 1997 Hilton Catt and Patricia Scudamore

All rights reserved. No part of this publication may be reproduced in any material form (including photocopying or storing it in any medium by electronic means and whether or not transiently or incidentally to some other use of this publication) without the written permission of the copyright owner, except in accordance with the provisions of the Copyright, Designs and Patents Act 1988 or under the terms of a licence issued by the Copyright Licensing Agency, 90 Tottenham Court Road, London W1P 9HE. Applications for the copyright owner's written permission to reproduce any part of this publication should be addressed to the publisher.

Distributed in the United States by
Sterling Publishing Co. Inc., 387 Park Avenue South, New York, NY 10016-8810

A British Library Cataloguing in Publication Data block for this book may be obtained from the British Library

ISBN 0 7063 7668 4

Design and typesetting Gwyn Lewis

Printed and bound in Great Britain by
Mackays of Chatham

Contents

Introduction: Setting the Scene 7
Quick quiz: ten questions to test your skills 11

1 Taking Stock of your Career 15
1.1 Deciding your next step 15
1.2 Deciding when to make a move 19
1.3 Considering career changes 26
1.4 Personal financial planning 30
1.5 Facing unemployment 31
Summary 32
Questions and answers 33

2 Putting Yourself on the Market 36
2.1 Applying for jobs you can do 36
2.2 Applying for jobs that exist 39
2.3 Targeting 42
2.4 Preparing a CV 48
2.5 Preparing yourself 60
Summary 64
Questions and answers 67

3 Making Applications 71
3.1 Finding out about jobs 71
3.2 Applying for the right jobs 87
3.3 Replying to advertisements 97
3.4 Applications for jobs sourced proactively 104
3.5 Keeping records of your applications 105

Summary 106
Questions and answers 109

4 GOING FOR INTERVIEWS 113
4.1 Not getting interviews 113
4.2 Types of interview 116
4.3 Preparing for interviews 119
4.4 Going to interviews 133
4.5 Preliminary interviews 138
4.6 Interviewers' questions 141
4.7 Closing interviews 149
4.8 After interviews 153
4.9 Having interviews and getting turned down 158
Summary 161
Questions and answers 163

5 GETTING JOBS 167
5.1 Offers of employment 167
5.2 Deciding to accept or decline 169
5.3 Accepting job offers 178
5.4 Turning jobs down 181
5.5 Working your notice 184
5.6 Relocation 187
5.7 Enticement (top jobs) 189
5.8 Starting a new job 191
Summary 195
Questions and answers 197

6 JOINING THE COMPLEMENTARY WORKFORCE 200
6.1 Temping 200
6.2 Contracts 204
6.3 Self-employment (freelancing) 206
Summary 213
Questions and answers 214

7 STARTING A CAREER 217
7.1 The market for first jobs in careers 217
7.2 Sourcing 220
7.3 Applying for your first career job 223
7.4 Applying for 'Trojan horse' jobs 225
Summary 229
Questions and answers 231

INDEX 234

Introduction: Setting the Scene

The world which faces people in careers, the real day-to-day world in which they have to make a living and carve out futures for themselves, has changed out of all recognition over the last 10–15 years. These changes have been dictated by a number of events:

- Recession, of course: the kind of economic conditions which have dogged us with brief respites since the early 1980s and which have wrought such havoc on traditional career structures, particularly in large firms.
- Increasing competitiveness in business; the emergence of a world market in which the customer calls the tune; in this situation the need to have costs firmly under control, including people costs.
- Shrinkage of the public sector.
- Emergence of small firms as important providers of quality employment. By the turn of the millennium over half the jobs in this country will be in firms which employ fewer than 50 people.
- Growth of short-term employment in various forms: contracts and temporary work as well as the increasing use of self-employed people to perform functions both in-house and on an outsourced basis. Collectively, these groups are referred to as the 'complementary workforce' (as opposed to the 'core work force': the permanent job holders).

- Growth of part-time employment.
- The end of soft landings for people who are seen as not succeeding; the general expectation these days that the price of failure is the sack, and that this applies at all levels.
- Rapid advances in technology (including the PC revolution); the greater risk of skills obsolescence.
- Abdication of responsibility for people's careers on the part of many employers; the view increasingly expressed that people should be responsible for their own careers.

Translated into effects on people's lives, these changes have meant:

- Fewer pairs of hands to do the work; more to do with fewer people to help; longer hours and no one to delegate mundane tasks to (tales of senior managers doing their own typing and making their own cups of coffee).
- Diminished job security (some would say no job security at all); the far greater likelihood these days that people will have to face up to redundancy at some point in their careers.
- Traditional career paths gone or truncated: once-familiar pyramids of management in bigger companies have frequently been broken up or squashed down; small firms by definition don't have much in the way of career paths.
- As a consequence of lost career paths, the death to a large extent of the one-company career: for the timid, the risk of being blocked in a dead end; for the ambitious, acceptance that getting on has to mean moving round; acceptance, too, that this can be risky.
- Some specialist functions obliterated altogether (witness the number of firms that don't have Human Resources Departments any more). For those affected, the need (albeit often unwelcome) to contemplate career changes or perhaps even to make the move into self-employment as a provider of outsourced services.
- Acceptance that modern careers are, at some point, much more likely to involve:

    – working for small firms;

- doing contracts/temporary assignments;
- being self-employed;
- working part-time or having a mix of part-time, temporary or self-employed jobs all at the same time (the classic portfolio worker).

- Acceptance that earnings will vary across the life span of a career; not assuming any more that pay is something which automatically goes up year on year (which, given good health and a clean copybook, could safely be taken as read with a traditional career); having to plan finances with contingencies in mind.

- Being well qualified, hardworking or good at what you do guarantees nothing.

- Getting into careers is harder; companies are less willing to carry learners; the difficulties this gives to newly qualified people and first job seekers (e.g. graduates).

- Careers aren't tidy any more; progress isn't always smooth or in one (upward) direction. As with earnings, there are going to be high spots and low spots, frequently with flat spots in between.

- Not relying on employers for career provision or career development; not relying on employers for updating skills either – in fact questioning what employers can deliver and, without necessarily being cynical, just how much they care.

One look at this list explains why many people in the 40-plus age group despair of the modern career situation and simply hanker for a return to the good old days. The sad fact, though, is that the good old days won't be coming back. Besides, a whole generation is now growing up who have never known what the good old days were like.

Sadly, too, the problems for people in careers don't stop there. Doing something about your career by seeking to change jobs is equally fraught with difficulty – so much so that a lot of people view the modern job market with considerable apprehension. In a survey we carried out recently, we asked job candidates to tell us what they found hardest to cope with. The following six factors emerged.

- The competition for any good job these days – the sheer volume of applications and the difficulty in even getting interviews.

- The treatment some employers dole out: the growing number of firms who don't reply to applications or let candidates know how they got on at interviews.

- The so-called invisible market. Is it true that over 90 per cent of jobs are never advertised? If so, how on earth does anyone ever access these jobs?

- The stigma of being too old or out of work (or both). The feeling of hopelessness for people who fall into these categories.

- The risks attached to changing jobs: the step into the unknown and the fear, when times get hard, that last in is usually first to go.

- The unwillingness on the part of many employers to offer training.

This book is about coming to terms with the modern career – how to exact what you want from unfavourable circumstances; how to perfect the art of the possible and use what's there; how to go one step further and discover the freedom and flexibility modern careers can offer.

The central message is this: having a career today means taking it into your own hands. It's you in charge (no one else) and you are the one responsible for giving your career the direction it needs. In turn, this means:

- You don't leave it to others to make the choices for you (they won't).

- You don't live in fantasy land. You are at all times realistic about what you can and can't achieve.

- You appreciate the risks. You know enough to keep yourself out of trouble.

- You unlearn the past and acquire a new set of survive-and-win skills.

Quick quiz: ten questions to test your skills

What would you do in each of these situations? Tick the statement which most closely approximates the course of action you would choose. The answers are given at the end of the Introduction.

Question 1
You wrote off for a job four weeks ago and received no reply, not even an acknowledgement. When you ring the firm's Personnel Department you are told the job has been filled. Do you:

A Ask why your application has been unsuccessful?
B Ask why they didn't let you know?
C Do a combination of A and B?
D Say thank you and goodbye (i.e. forget it)?
E Write to the firm's Managing Director and complain about the shoddy treatment?

Question 2
You hear about a good job. You also hear there have been over 400 applicants. Do you:

A Apply anyway?
B Take the view you don't stand a chance and give it a miss?
C Ring in and say you will only apply if you can be guaranteed an interview?
D Wait for the queue to die down and send off your application after a couple of weeks?
E Hand-deliver your application ?

Question 3
You narrowly miss getting a good job (you end up in the last two). Do you:

A Ring up the firm as quickly as possible and tell them they've made the wrong choice?
B Blame the interviewer?
C Accept the decision and leave it at that?
D Accept the decision, but ring up a fortnight later to see if the successful candidate has accepted?

E Write, saying you are disappointed but thanking the firm for considering you?

Question 4
You see a good job advertised. You meet all the requirements except you are not in the age bracket stated (you are eight years too old). Do you:

A Take the view that applying will be a waste of time?
B Phone in first and try to find out if the company is prepared to be flexible?
C Leave your age out of your application?
D Apply anyway?
E Put a covering letter with your application saying you realise you are too old but emphasising in what other ways you are qualified?

Question 5
Twelve months ago you applied for a job with a big company. You had a preliminary interview and got turned down. You see the same company advertising again. Do you:

A Feel there is no point in applying?
B Ring up first?
C Put a covering letter with your application to remind them they have seen you before?
D Write off and make no mention of your previous application?
E Write a brief letter referring to your previous application, and leave it to them to let you know if they want to see you again?

Question 6
You see a job advertised which looks good, but there is no mention of salary. Do you:

A Apply anyway, with the intention of sorting out the salary if and when you get to an interview?
B Ring up and try to find out?
C Give the job a miss?
D Apply, making it clear what you are earning now and what you are looking for?

E   Write in to say the job looks interesting, but you won't be applying unless you know what the salary is?

Question 7

You are a Marketing Assistant. The firm you work for is going through a major restructuring exercise. As part of this exercise you are told the Marketing Department is going to close and your job will no longer be available. As an alternative to redundancy, the firm is prepared to offer you a job as PA to the Operations Manager on the same salary and subject to the same terms and conditions as those which apply to your current job. You have, however, always seen your career in marketing and you are not sure if you want to make a switch. If you take redundancy it will be worth about £1,500 to you. Do you:

A   Turn the offer down and take the redundancy terms?
B   Try the new job out for 12 months?
C   Find out what's happening to the marketing work?
D   Take the new job, but start making applications for jobs in marketing straight away?
E   Take the new job, but ask for a payment to compensate you for the loss of your career?

Question 8

You are offered a job by XYZ Limited and you hand in your notice. Two weeks later XYZ Limited write to you again to say they have changed their minds and the offer is withdrawn. At first your present employer is reluctant to allow you to retract your notice, but finally they agree. You are left with the feeling, though, that there is a big cloud hanging over your head. Do you:

A   Write to XYZ Limited, seeking some kind of compensation?
B   Accept the situation and do nothing further?
C   Look for another job in earnest?
D   Engage a firm of solicitors to start legal proceedings against XYZ?
E   View the experience as a lesson and take yourself off the employment market altogether?

Question 9

You have been offered a really good job with a really good firm. However, one of the terms is that you agree to 12 months' notice, and you realise this will clearly impede your chances of ever getting another job. Do you:

A Turn the offer down?
B Seek to re-negotiate the 12 months' notice down to three?
C View the requirement as perfectly reasonable and accept the offer happily?
D Ask for more money to recompense you for the loss of employment opportunities?
E Ask for the 12 months' notice to come in after a trial period?

Question 10

You want promotion but in the firm you work for the best jobs always seem to go to people they bring in from outside. Do you?

A Complain?
B Blame yourself for not making your ambitions known?
C Keep quiet and start looking for another job?
D See how things go over the next couple of years?
E Accept that you are not promotion material?

How did you get on?

The answers we're looking for are:

Question 1 **D**
Question 2 **A**
Question 3 **D** (**E** is acceptable)
Question 4 **E** (**D** is acceptable)
Question 5 **D**
Question 6 **D**
Question 7 **C** then **B** (in that order)
Question 8 **A** and **C** combined
Question 9 **C**
Question 10 **B**

Now read the book and find out why.

ONE

TAKING STOCK OF YOUR CAREER

Because of the way things are today, a lot of people in careers find themselves drifting round aimlessly and not achieving what they really want to achieve. Occasionally this aimlessness leads them into trouble. A bit like ships with no power, no rudders and no charts, they end up going nowhere and leave themselves entirely at the mercy of the stormy seas.

What we plan to do in this first chapter is to cure you of any aimlessness by getting you to take stock of your career and be clear about where you are now and where you are going.

1.1 Deciding your next step

Career power starts with options:

- realising you've got options (always);
- knowing how and when to use your options.

Options aren't the same for everybody. The range of options you have, what you can and can't do, depends on how much risk you can take – and, in turn, on your commitments and circumstances. If, for example, you happen to be out of work, and not responsible for supporting anyone except yourself, you may be able to entertain the option of working on a week-by-week basis for someone you know to be a three-times bankrupt. You'll be off your head to do the same if it involves having to give up a regular job with a regular income when you've got a family and a mortgage to provide for.

Options for people in careers tend to fall under three broad headings:

- staying put (trying to achieve what you want to achieve internally);
- moving on (finding another job – or another career);
- moving into the complementary sector: working for yourself or on short-term contracts.

We have listed these three headings in what most people see as the ascending order of risk, but this isn't necessarily the way it goes. Staying put in a declining industry is, for a start, decidedly risky. Not only will you be running the risk of ending up on a redundancy list, but your skills will become obsolete too.

To see how this assessing of risks and options works in practice, let's use a case study.

> Tom is a Senior Quantity Surveyor with a medium-sized construction company. Like most firms in construction, Tom's employer has been through lean times in the last few years and only recently have things started to pick up. Tom's problem is that he is still on the same salary as he was on three years ago – this being the last time anyone had a rise. What's more, Tom is running the QS Department practically single-handedly, his only support being a trainee. Previously, Tom had two fully qualified surveyors working under him. One of these was made redundant when the firm hit a particularly bad patch, and the other wasn't replaced when she left. This situation was all well and good when work was slack, but Tom is now finding he is working six and sometimes seven days a week. Because he is on the senior staff payroll, he is not paid for his additional hours.
>
> Tom's boss, the Contracts Director, has told Tom the company's cash position is still perilous and, until jobs have been completed and money starts to come in, there is no chance of the Board

> sanctioning extra staff. Tom hasn't bothered asking about his salary – he figures he knows what answer he will get.
>
> Tom is now weighing up his options. He is 34 and he has been with this firm eight years. Finding another job with better pay and more regular hours seems the obvious solution, but Tom's concern is the risk he will be taking. The construction industry is notorious for its ups and downs, and Tom realises moving jobs means not only venturing into the unknown but also putting himself in the position of 'last in'.
>
> Tom is married with three young children and a mortgage to provide for. His wife works part-time as a supply teacher but Tom is very much the breadwinner.

Does Tom's situation sound familiar?

The problem for people like Tom, people who see their capacity to take risks as limited, is they usually end up shutting-up and staying-put because they don't see they have any other option.

This is mistake number one and the cause of much misery.

Every option has a risk to it, including the shutting-up and staying-put option. In Tom's case, shutting-up and staying-put means carrying on working for a firm with self-confessed liquidity problems – and in an industry with a high incidence of corporate failure. Nor is Tom convinced things will improve for him – meaning he is running the further risk of continuing to work long hours for what he sees as poor reward. And what will the effect of this be on him and his family, in both the short term and long term?

The good news, though, for the Toms of this world is that they usually have more in the way of options than they think. Furthermore, with a little thought and organisation, they can often extend their options by extending their capacity to take risks (more on this in a moment).

Let's see first if we can think up a few options for Tom apart from suffering in silence. He will, of course, make a far better job of doing this himself (he knows his own situation best).

- We know help for Tom in the form of extra staff has been turned down, but what about some financial recognition for all the long hours he's putting in? The firm may not be happy about paying him for overtime if it sets a precedent for other senior people, but how about a one-off bonus or, better for them perhaps, a bonus payable as and when the cash for respective jobs comes in? Risks for Tom? – none as far as we can see (they can always say no).

- The modern job market with all its pitfalls is a subject we will be devoting a lot of space to in this book. But, while Tom is right to be wary about swapping jobs, there are, as we shall see, ways and means of minimising risk and avoiding bad moves. In short, Tom should be including shopping the market on his list of options. The *quid pro quo* is he makes himself good at it.

- Tom might be able to strike a deal with his firm in which he goes freelance (self-employed) while they retain him to do their surveying (either in-house or outsourced). If the price is right, the advantages for Tom are:

    – he gets paid for what he does;
    – it's up to him to decide whether he drafts in any help.

In Chapter 6 we will be looking at freelancing and ways and means of minimising the risks of becoming self-employed, but for now don't dismiss it as an option just for chancers. Also, with freelancing, there is the opportunity to find other sources of work and income, thereby reducing the risk of being tied to the fortunes of one firm (a good point for Tom).

Structuring options
Options can be structured. By this we mean you can try them one at a time and in the order they appeal to you. Tom, for example, can try squeezing a bit more money out of his firm first, then, if that doesn't work, move on to exploring the outside market, and so on.

Extending your options
We have seen the strong link between availability of options and capacity to take risks. Whereas it is easy to see how you can restrict your options by saddling yourself with big overheads, the

reverse is also true. You can enhance your range of options and ultimately your career power by careful management of incomings and outgoings. Using Tom as the example again, he will be able to be far more adventurous if his family has less dependence on his earnings. This brings into question his wife's earnings. Can she do more hours or even get a full-time job? Will Tom be able to facilitate this by spending less time at work and providing more help with family chores? Will this in turn be easier for him if he works freelance?

This also illustrates how couples and families – people with commitments who tend to see themselves as low risk-takers – have the ability to apportion risk between themselves. One partner in a relationship can, for example, be the risk-taker while the other plays ultra-safe. At certain times, and depending on career situations, these roles can be switched about.

Beyond the next step

What about longer-term ambitions and career destinations? Where do these fit in?

While there's nothing wrong with setting yourself an aim such as getting on the Board of Directors by the time you're 35, what is important at all times in this funny world we live in is to retain your *flexibility*. This means don't rule out options simply because they don't fit into your grand plan. Instead, always be prepared to look at what's on offer and weigh it up for what it's worth. Be prepared, too, to change your mind about where you see yourself going in both the short and long term. Sometimes, these days, the way to reach your career destination is via a dog-leg route.

Being inflexible is a particular danger for the unemployed and those facing unemployment (more on this later).

1.2 Deciding when to make a move

Though one-company careers are by no means defunct, there is an increasing likelihood today that you will need to change jobs from time to time to advance your career in the direction you want it to go. Deciding when your career with your present employer has run out of steam is what we will be looking at next.

• WARNING •

People with too many voluntary job moves on their CVs are viewed with suspicion by employers. Job-hopping is seen as evidence that 'here we have someone who can't settle down' or 'someone who can't fit in', and – with the emphasis very much on team working these days – it creates a definite negative point against your selection. The message is this: don't make job moves just for the sake of them, just because you feel like a change. Unless your job is under threat or your circumstances are particularly unbearable, see a move as something which advances your career. In other words, make your job moves count.

Another way of viewing job moves is that the number you can make without blotting your copybook is limited.

Grudges and grouses

Most of us like a good moan now and then, but usually this is as far as it goes. Sometimes, however, dissatisfaction is the reason why people feel the need to start shopping around. The premise they are working on is that there is something better for them out there.

A lot of the annoyances and frustrations people face these days can be put down to the kind of post-recessionary conditions described in the Introduction. Our overworked and underpaid friend Tom is a good example of someone dissatisfied because his firm has been through hard times.

Tom may well be able to find himself a better-paid job with fewer hours, but there is something he needs to consider before jumping in too quickly: will he be using up one of his limited number of job changes on a move which, in career terms, could turn out to be sideways? How much better it would be for Tom if he could look to broader issues, like where his career is going and what the market might be able to offer him in terms of real advancement. The underlying point here is that resolving a grievance or a number of grievances shouldn't be the only criterion you use in targeting your next job.

One of the snags about moving sideways is that you can go on moving sideways, i.e. you can keep changing jobs with no real advancement. This won't look good on your CV.

Career paths wiped out

Another post-recession phenomenon is the emergence of so-called flat organisations – ones in which the traditional pyramid-shaped structure of management jobs has been done away with by a process known as 'de-layering'. People who work in flat organisations (the survivors) have seen their career paths taken away. If you work in a flat organisation:

- Don't wait to be told it's time to make a move. Remember it's you in the driving seat.
- Don't hang round waiting for the pyramids to return (they won't).

Being passed by

Seeing promotion chances offered to others and not to you is, on the face of it, a good enough reason for thinking the time has come to start looking around. Seeing promotion chances offered to outsiders seems an even stronger signal to go.

Ironically, perhaps, one of the most frequent complaints we get from companies is that none of their staff seem to want to take on extra responsibilities. Yet, in most cases, these are staff who haven't actually been asked. The presumption is that staff who want to get on should make a point of bringing the matter up.

Here is where the impasse arises. People, particularly people in careers, feel awkward about going along to the boss and saying 'I want to get on. I don't want to be doing this same job in two years' time', because it smacks of grousing. Sadly, though, the consequence of this silence is that companies look outside for candidates for good jobs – and of course there is nothing more infuriating for ambitious people than seeing their promotion avenues taken over by newcomers.

The first point to impress on you is that stating your ambitions isn't grousing. The message you need to be putting across is: 'I like it here, and I enjoy my work, but at some stage I want to use my experience and qualifications to get me a more responsible job.' Apart from being perfectly respectable, putting your objectives on the table like this is giving your employer a chance. The company may or may not be able to offer you promotion, but at least the subject is opened up. Faced with this kind of candidness, companies have the opportunity to be candid back. With luck, they will tell you how they view your chances, and how they see your career developing.

Waiting 30 years for the boss to retire and hoping the company in its infinite wisdom will see fit to put you into his or her shoes isn't what most people these days would view as being wildly ambitious. But, if your employer in response to your statement tells you that your prospects for promotion are good, and if you have no reason to disbelieve your employer, then the sensible thing would be to 'stick with it' but mentally set a time limit – say two years.

From around 25 to 38 years of age is the period when you are most upwardly mobile, and you must not squander these years. If your employer does not deliver within your set time period, or if you see bad signs (like outsiders being brought in to do the jobs you would like to do), then it's high time to get some options open. But the point in giving your present employer the chance to offer you promotion is twofold:

- You know the company (warts and all), whereas moving into the big outside world means moving into the unknown, i.e. more risk for you.
- The company knows you. They will be promoting you because they have confidence in your abilities. They will tend to back their judgement by being more supportive of you than a new employer would be.

Career paths blocked

Some companies, by definition probably the better ones, have a low turnover of people at the top. The result is a promotion bottleneck: not enough opportunities for all the bright young people coming up through the ranks. If you are in this situation, then if you want to get on you've got to get out. Again, don't wait to be told.

Too long in the job

Once upon a time long service with a firm was considered good. It went with enhanced job security, a good retirement pension and maybe a gold watch after 25 years. The sad fact, though, is that it is no longer necessarily in your best interests to attach yourself to one employer for long periods. In job-market terms, you can become devalued and have less to offer another employer. You can even start to under-achieve.

Comfortable and happy though your present existence may seem, it is still going to pay you to keep in touch with the outside world. Don't wait for disgruntlement or the threat of redundancy to come along. Test the temperature of the water once in a while and see what's out there, because it can benefit you greatly and it certainly does no harm. You can, for example, find out if you are being underpaid or if the market wants people with skills you haven't got (e.g. in areas of new technology). It will alert you to take steps to acquire these skills and keep your market value intact.

As a guide, everyone who is not within ten years of retiring should be putting themselves on the market every five years (minimum). This is one of the golden rules for the new age of careers. In this way, and this way only, will you keep yourself in touch with what's going on. It will also act as a kind of catch-all which will pull you up short if, for any reason, you are procrastinating about career decisions or allowing your career to stagnate.

Working in small firms

The issue of small firms – working for small firms, applying for jobs in small firms – will crop up time and time again in this book.

Small firms are already playing an increasingly important part in people's careers and this trend is set to continue.

One of the snags with working in a small firm is the prospects. This is a question not just of size but also of who owns the firm. Small firms tend to be private companies. The people they belong to are the people who run them (the partners or the directors if the firm is a limited liability company). It is usual for the equity in small firms to be jealously guarded and outsiders – unless they happen to be particularly faithful and long-serving retainers – will find it hard to aspire to directorships or partnerships.

There is an up side, though, to working in small firms, and this is the experience you get. Job functions tend to be broad and flexible, so there is an opportunity to widen your skills. There is a new breed of small firm on the scene too. These have come about either through hiving-off and management buy-outs or from fresh starts by former big-company people (casualties of the purges, maybe). The difference with this new breed of small firm is they are professionally as opposed to entrepreneurially run.

Verdict on small firms?

If you happen to be working in one, don't just view it as a stopgap. See what you can gain from the experience, but always be aware of your situation and keep in touch with the big wide world outside.

As a footnote to working in small firms and deciding whether it's time to move on, be mindful of the fact that many successful small firms aren't in static situations. Where the ownership is forward-thinking and adventurous, the firm may be going for growth and here the ground rules are different. Don't, whatever you do, jump off the ship just as it's about to set sail.

Seeing the writing on the wall

If you feel for any reason that your job is at risk, you must get yourself out on the job market without delay. Getting yourself into a good job is much harder if you are unemployed. People who have been out of work for long periods know this to their cost.

Telling you to avoid unemployment sounds like a bad joke, but there are plenty of people around who intentionally put themselves out of a job. These are not just people who take voluntary redundancy. They include people who can see the writing on the wall but do nothing about it.

Anticipating redundancy isn't just a question of being aware how your employer is performing and how your employer's customers are performing; there are other danger signs which flash up from time to time.

- Someone new arrives at the top (Chief Executive or Managing Director). Rest assured, things are going to change, and don't be surprised if a few heads start to roll. Take particular note if you are part of the senior management.

- Your firm is taken over or merged with another business. Mergers and acquisitions are usually accompanied by restructurings and reorganisations, meaning that jobs will disappear somewhere along the line.

- If you work in the public sector, you are told that the service you are involved in is going to be put out to competitive tendering. This means you could find yourself working for a private-sector supplier. Expect redundancies to follow.

- Your firm announces it is going to invest in new technology. New technology unfortunately tends to mean fewer jobs. Firms with the money to invest in new technology will be firms who are doing well and where jobs would otherwise be secure – hence job losses come when employees are expecting them least.

In any of these situations you need to be opening up your options.

Of course redundancy isn't the only reason people find themselves without a job. There are other situations which also spell out danger.

- You get a new boss (someone you don't know). You have no idea how the two of you are going to get on. Most of the time everything works out fine, but human relationships are funny and there is always the risk of some kind of personality clash developing.

- You have been given warnings about some aspect of your job performance. Be especially wary if you can't see any real reason why you are being singled out.

- Your attendance record is impaired by sickness or family problems. Small firms with a lot of commercial pressures on them find absence particularly hard to cope with.

1.3 Considering career changes

Complete changes of career tend to figure in people's aspirations when they are in one of the following two situations.

- Fed up with what they are doing and wanting to do something else. We call these visionary career changes.

- In a forced situation, where changing career is a matter of necessity.

Visionary career changes

Most of us go through periods when we view our jobs as humdrum and unexciting. Usually these phases pass, but for some the urge to seek out more fulfilling things to do in life doesn't go away.

> John is a Tooling Engineer. He is 33, married with two children and earning £25,000 a year. John has decided he wants to get into sales. Spending the rest of his life on the factory floor doesn't appeal any more. He wants to be out and about meeting people.
>
> John's wife is fully supportive. She wants him happy and 'getting on'. Last year John did a correspondence course. Now he has a Diploma in Salesmanship. Six months ago John started applying for sales jobs. He had a nice CV prepared and wrote off for about 40 jobs. The result, however, was disappointing. In most cases he did not even receive a reply. Only on one occasion did he get as far as an interview. At this (to his utter dismay) he was told that because of his lack of experience he could only be viewed as a trainee and that the starting salary for trainees was less than £8,000 a year. John explained about his commitments (mortgage, etc.) and how he could not afford to take such a huge drop in pay.

> John is now totally dejected. It seems no one will give him a chance with his career change – not unless he's prepared to work for peanuts. So much for all the long hours of study and trying hard. It simply isn't fair.

Though he doesn't know it, John's experiences are fairly typical. Employment these days is highly competitive and, in applying for sales jobs, John is competing against people with proven sales' track records. Hence it is hardly surprising that his applications keep ending up on the 'not selected for interview' pile.

But does this mean people shouldn't have ambitions and want to do things which will make them happier and improve their lives?

Of course not. The message is simply this – changing career, swapping horses in midstream, is notoriously difficult and potentially quite painful. It's far easier to carry on in the line of work in which you have experience. But because something is difficult doesn't mean you shouldn't do it. What it does mean, however, is steeling yourself for the knocks; understanding you are doing something which is highly speculative and where the odds are stacked against you; appreciating most of all that to achieve what you want to achieve may take a very long time.

There is the risk element to consider, too. Who knows how successful you are going to be in your new career? What if you only last a few weeks? What will you do if the worst happens? These are all reasons for questioning your motives and your commitment very closely indeed. As part of this questioning, go back to your options. In particular, ask yourself if your urge to change career has simply come about because you've been in the job too long, in which case a more straightforward and less risky route for you would be just to change jobs (i.e. stay in the same career but work for someone else).

Going back to John, what he really needs to do is re-examine his commitment to getting into sales. A fall in earnings is usually on the cards when you swap careers. You can't expect to hop from one ladder onto another without dropping a few rungs or even having to go back to ground level. This is something he and his wife need to consider. Maybe Mrs John has to take on board the idea of getting a part-time job so they can make ends meet while John is getting established in his new career. Maybe it will be several years before John starts pulling in £25,000 a year again. They need a contingency plan too: life in sales can be nasty, brutish and short for those who don't make the grade. Fortunately, John can go back to being a Tooling Engineer, which is some security if he should find himself out on his ear.

Of course we could criticise John for not finding out more about the rocky road ahead before he started along it. But we don't live in a perfect world, and most of us learn our lessons from experience. The important thing, though, is to use our experiences: to listen to what we are being told and to modify our plans accordingly, even when what we are being told is something we would rather not hear. John, unfortunately, has taken umbrage at being told he will have to start as a trainee. He has treated the information as a personal affront and, in consequence, will probably ignore the feedback and gather nothing from his experience.

Forced career changes

This is a different kettle of fish altogether and usually brought about by changed personal or economic circumstances. Two examples are:

- Stella, whose career in professional sport has been brought to an end by a back injury.
- Craig, who has been a Mining Engineer all his life. The pits in the area have all been shut down and he doesn't want to move.

Here are a few pointers for people facing forced career changes.

- Start by examining the transferability of your skills and experience. Does your knowledge and experience lend itself to any other kind of work? Could Stella, for example, look at going into retailing sports equipment? Could Craig's skills and experience be applied to, say, selling mechanical handling plant?
- Proceed with a profound sense of realism. Be prepared to start at

rock bottom, but take heart from the fact that your skills and experience ought to put you on a fast track so you won't be there long.

- Allied to realism, look at what you can do to gear your finances to accommodate lower earnings in the short term. Do you, for example, have a spouse/partner who can take on more of the financial burden? Can you cut down on any of your outgoings? (Also see section 1.4 below.)

- Be prepared for none of this to be easy. As with John, steel yourself for the knocks and keep reminding yourself you are trying to do something (change career) which is intrinsically difficult.

- Keep going.

Toe-dipping

An idea for you, if you are contemplating a career change, is to dip your toe in the water before you dive in at the deep end. Two possible ways of doing this are:

- Use your own time. For example, Fiona is a secretary who fancies becoming a teacher, teaching word-processing and office skills. Fiona spent last year attending evening classes to get her teaching qualifications. Now she intends to try teaching first-hand by getting a class one night a week at the local evening institute. If this works out, she will apply for full-time teaching jobs next year. In the mean time she is keeping her secretarial job.

- Take a week's holiday and offer your services to someone free.

This is a case of hedging your bets by not giving up your day job until you're quite certain you're making the right move.

Facilitating career changes

With modern careers you can never be quite certain when the need to make a change may *either* suit your purposes *or* be forced upon you. One way you can enhance your ability to make career changes is by keeping your skills base:

- as wide as possible;
- up-to-date.

We mentioned earlier that working in small firms provides an excellent opportunity for broadening skills. Similarly, in companies which have been through bad times, people and sometimes whole functions have been axed and the responsibilities pushed onto those remaining. This is an example of how something which on the face of it appears bad (more work to do for no more pay) can in the long run turn to your advantage.

1.4 Personal financial planning

We have seen already how sensible financial provision can:

- enhance your risk-taking ability and, in turn, the range of options you have at your disposal;
- enable you to make career changes.

With a traditional career, it was safe to assume that earnings went up year on year. Generally speaking, the longer you stuck at it the better off you became – and you could gear up your standard of living on the basis of this predictability. This is not so with modern careers, which don't go in one direction only. These days, earnings can vary enormously from one year to the next and you have to make provision for rainy days.

There are two extremes of conduct here. Whereas having a bumper year and blowing the lot on a new car and restocking the wine cellar may not be the sensible thing to do, neither is stashing everything away in the bank and living the life of a pauper. You need to reap some benefit for all your hard work; enjoying yourself and having a bit of fun is important. Don't go over the top, that's all.

Fully flexible finances (FFF)

What would help you is if some of your outgoings (your costs) could be made to go up and down in line with your incomings. Some items in your budget (such as council tax and utilities' bills) won't respond to this kind of treatment, but others can be made to. For example, contributions to personal pension plans can be varied. Fully flexible financing can also be achieved by a bit of self-conditioning. You can condition yourself into accepting that the kind of holiday you can afford will vary from one year to another. View this as part of the fun of managing your own career.

One aspect of FFF we have touched on already is where you have a spouse or partner whose earnings can be made to contribute to a greater or lesser extent, depending on need. The increased availability of temporary and part-time employment helps here.

Gearing

If you are going through a period where your earnings are particularly volatile or where, for example, you may want to spend some money on marketing yourself as a freelancer, there is no harm in looking (as a fully fledged business might) at taking on short-term borrowings. Obviously you need to be sensible about this and to make sure you are not just funding overspending. What we are saying here is that negotiating a small overdraft facility with your friendly local bank is preferable to cutting down on life's basics.

Pensions

Exercising options – changing jobs, spending periods of time in temporary and/or self-employment – has been greatly facilitated by the advent of the portable personal pension. No longer are you forced to join employers' (occupational) schemes. You can make your own pension arrangements, contribute at the levels you see fit, which you can vary, and take your pension with you wherever you decide to go to. This contrasts with reaching retiring age with a ragbag of frozen pensions from various previous employers' occupational schemes.

1.5 Facing unemployment

Once you have digested what we said earlier about seeing the writing on the wall and avoiding unemployment, what happens if you do have the bad luck to find yourself out of work? How does being unemployed affect the way in which you take stock?

One of the few good things going for unemployed people is that they can afford to take risks (what have they got to lose?). This has the effect of putting a very wide range of options at their disposal. For example, making career changes and moving into self-employment will be far easier decisions for people who are unemployed.

Surprisingly, though, many newly unemployed people (consciously or not) only consider one option – finding a job like the job they just lost. This means they often rule out the option of short-term complementary-sector employment when (as we shall see later in the book) temping in one form or another can prove to be a very useful stepping-stone back into a permanent job.

The message to unemployed people is this – use your ability to take risks to allow you to take full advantage of what's on offer in the market place. Explore all options and don't rule any out.

Summary

There is a tendency on the part of many people to view the modern career market as a 'bad' place. The reasons are entirely understandable. There is another view, though: the view that people in careers today enjoy far more freedom and flexibility than their predecessors did 15, 20 and 30 years ago. How come?

When you think about it, the traditional career was very much managed for you. If you didn't like the way it was being managed, your only real option was to leave and find someone else who might manage it better. Managing your own career – determining your own objectives and the path you are going to go along – is, in our view, infinitely better than having someone else do it for you, and running the risk that they may do it badly. Under-achieve today and you've only got yourself to blame!

One of the great plus points of modern careers is their diversity. The emergence of small firms and the breaking-down of many of the big monoliths of the past into smaller constituents has introduced a choice, a range of options, which wasn't there before. As firms have sought to make themselves more flexible, the growth of the complementary sector has brought a further dimension into play.

Getting the best for yourself out of this diversity is what career power is all about. The opportunities to move round and mix 'n' match are enormous but what you've got to decide first is what's for you in all this diversity and what isn't: your options linked to your ability to take risks.

Risk understandably bothers people, but there is a world of difference between assessing risk properly and being driven by fear. The way to conquer fear is by gaining knowledge. The way to gain knowledge is by getting out there and seeing what's happening. Don't run away from risk. Don't let it frighten you. Don't see your options, either, in terms of safe havens and shark-infested waters. As a rule of thumb in this world of modern careers, nothing is ever as safe as or as dangerous as it first seems.

Finally, never see your situation as hopeless. This goes especially for people who have been out of work a long time or who see themselves as 'too old' or otherwise disadvantaged. The diversity of the modern market has much to offer people who fall into categories which have been hitherto viewed as 'difficult'.

Questions and answers

Moving jobs means loss of pension rights

Q *I am 45, been with one company for 18 years and very conscious I am under-achieving. What bothers me most about changing jobs is my pension. If I leave, the choices are to have it frozen or to transfer it to my new employer's scheme. As I see it, either way I will lose quite badly in terms of my final pension. What's the answer to this?*

A Generally speaking, occupational pension schemes are structured to benefit members who stick the course and go through to normal retiring age. Hence, in terms of frozen pensions and transfer values, people who leave feel they get rough deals. One point you need to consider though is that most occupational schemes are based on final salary and, if you are right (i.e. if you are underachieving) then your final salary with a new employer is going to be a lot better than if you stay where you are. Think about it!

Options and age

Q *I am 54 and in a job which I don't like and which I took as a stopgap when I got made redundant three years ago. I would like to think I've got options, but at my age is this being realistic?*

A You've always got options. First, the job market is not as hostile to over-50s as you may think and, second, the growth of the complementary sector has given a big boost to the job prospects of people in their last 15 years. Roughly speaking, no one will care how old you are if you're coming in to do a short-term assignment or provide some service on a freelance basis. The only criterion will be: can you do the job?

Change of career as an alternative to redundancy

Q *I am a Human Resources Manager and my firm has just announced they are going to close the HR Department. I can take redundancy if I want to but I have been offered an alternative job, on the same salary, running one of the firm's small depots. I must admit my first reaction is to say no – mainly because I view Human Resources Management as my career – but how do you think I should play this?*

A Do you know what your firm intends to do with the HR function? In short, is there any chance they could outsource it to you if you set yourself up as a freelance HR consultant? If there is, you could add it on to your list of options. Other than this, you could try the depot management job for, say, 12 months and see how it goes. Why?

- It avoids redundancy/unemployment.
- You might find you like it.

- If it doesn't work out, you can still revert to applying for jobs in HR.
- It gives you the opportunity to broaden your skills (even more options).

Small firms are risky

Q *I work for a large multinational and I have always been wary of small firms because in my view they can't ever hope to offer the same level of job security. As someone with a lot of personal commitments (children in private schools, etc.), am I right to give small firms a wide berth?*

A True, small firms don't have the financial underpinnings of huge multinationals, but don't fall into the trap of viewing your present situation as riskless. What happens to you if, for example, Mr Big in Bologna decides to shift whatever the UK operation does out to the Pacific rim? In contrast, the people who own small businesses have their livelihoods wrapped up in them and will usually go to enormous lengths to keep them going.

TWO

Putting Yourself on the Market

We will now take a look at what you need to consider before you start applying for jobs. The job market has changed substantially in recent years, and you need to make sure you're ready to face it.

2.1 Applying for jobs you can do

There was the tale from a few years back of the office boy who idled away his time thumbing through the 'Situations Vacant' column of the *Daily Telegraph* and writing off for any Managing Director's job which chanced to catch his eye. You may not be in quite the same league as our whimsical office boy, but the first thing you need to check is that you are applying for jobs you can do. This sounds so obvious – yet there are a surprising number of people around who invest enormous amounts of time and effort into applying for jobs they don't stand a chance of getting.

The time-wasting in itself isn't so bad, but what does the damage is the procession of 'No thank you' letters they end up getting. The disappointment and the feeling of rejection and failure sooner or later get through. These turn into resentment and frustration, and finally into the conviction that everyone out there is against them and, for some reason, can't appreciate their talents.

If you find you don't even get interviews, then there is a good chance you may be falling into the trap of applying for jobs you can't do. Because of the way recruitment works, no one tells you this. All you get back are those brief, unhelpful, pre-printed or word-processed letters saying 'No' and 'Sorry'. A Career Counsellor might put you right – or a friendly face at an employment agency – but the likelihood is that you will carry on lurching from job application to job application, getting more and more despondent, until finally you give up because you feel you can't take any more. The best hope you've got is to realise for yourself that the jobs you are applying for are a complete mismatch for your skills, experience and qualifications.

To help you with this bit of self-analysis, we have assembled some of the more typical situations in which people find themselves applying for jobs they can't do. See if any of these have a familiar ring (be honest with yourself).

Taking a step too far . . .

These days, there are a lot of pressures to succeed. Such pressures frequently lead people into the trap of over-reaching. They try to go too far, too fast – and inevitably the results are disappointing.

> Marcella is a Product Designer. She has worked in the Design Office of a plastics company for over five years. She is now 28 and has her sights set on getting into a management position by the time she is 30. She is well qualified (degree in industrial design) and feels she has all the necessary attributes. She is even working towards a postgraduate Diploma in Management Studies, which she is doing in her own time. Marcella has been applying for any design management positions she has seen advertised in the press. The results so far have not been encouraging: 17 applications, two interviews only, and in both cases she did not get shortlisted. Marcella has already twigged that the big problem is her lack of management experience. Some of the ads she has replied to did actually stipulate 'at least five years experience in a management position', or words to that effect. To Marcella, all this seems faintly ridiculous – how is she supposed to get experience if no one gives her a chance?

The writing is on the wall for Marcella. Pretty soon she will get discouraged and give up. This is a pity because Marcella is perfectly right to have her eyes on a management job. Anything less and she would not be doing justice to herself. The difficulty for Marcella is that these days companies don't take chances with people – the downsides are too big for them. With people they don't know (i.e. people coming in from outside) they will stick with the tried-and-tested, and give preference to those who have experience. Putting learners into key positions is too potentially troublesome for them, and it is a risk that they needn't take – so they won't.

There are a lot of Marcellas about: people, young people in the main, who are well qualified, hardworking, highly motivated and who find the doors slamming in their faces.

So what should Marcella do? In the first place – if she has not already done so – she should make her ambitions known to her present employer along the lines we suggested earlier, when we looked at how to handle being passed by for promotion. The point, you remember, is that making upward moves is usually easier if done internally. But, once Marcella has exhausted the internal route, she may have to start to look at what the world outside has to offer.

Here a stratagem she could try is 'moving sideways now to move upwards later' – in other words, move sideways to a firm who will be in a position to offer her the prospect of promotion. She could, for example, apply for a Product Designer's job in a bigger firm.

Should Marcella stop applying for design management jobs? Certainly not – for the simple reason that she could strike lucky. At the end of the day, selection is down to one person's view of another. Someone, somewhere, may just take a shine to her – and that is all it takes. But what Marcella must remember (rather like John the Tooling Engineer and his career change) is that these are speculative applications where the odds are stacked against her, and therefore she shouldn't get wound up by the turn-downs. Rather, she should treat them as the norm.

Not reading advertisements properly

This is a common problem. Some people have a way of reading job advertisements and skipping over anything in the requirements which rules them out. They may do this knowingly ('Let's give it a whirl, what the hell!') or, in their anxiety to get off an application for a good job, they may not actually notice the bit that says 'must be familiar with JIT techniques' or 'must speak French'. Again, the damage is done by the turn-down letters that arrive on the doormat several weeks later when most people will have forgotten the finer points of the job specification (whether they noticed them in the first place or not). The whole episode gets viewed with the usual mixture of dejection and annoyance which puts people on the slippery slope to discouragement.

If you stay detached and don't get wound up about the turn-downs, there is no harm in applying for jobs where you don't quite meet all the requirements, providing (this is important) the jobs meet yours. Sometimes employers assemble such formidable lists of desirable qualifications, skills and experiences that they end up with no one who has all the attributes, but instead get a lot of near misses. Here is where you might get your chance.

2.2 Applying for jobs that exist

Make sure you are applying for jobs that are available on the market. Beware of looking for jobs that only exist in your mind.

> Roger is an Electrical Engineer. Roger is 24 and still working for the bakery company where he served his apprenticeship. Roger is engaged and plans to get married next year, which means that he and his fiancée have been discussing mortgages. Roger's salary is £15,000 a year, though he can make this up to £18,000 with overtime, He is not, however, keen on working overtime because he plays for a local football team, which means training two nights a week and matches on Saturday during the season.
>
> Roger has figured that the way out of his dilemma is to get a job as a Commissioning Engineer, preferably working on bakery plant

where his skills and experience are ideal. He has spoken to a couple of Commissioning Engineers he knows. They earn £25,000 a year, plus all sorts of allowances and bonuses. With this kind of money, Roger realises he won't have to worry about overtime.

Roger starts by putting together a list of all the manufacturers of bakery equipment in the area and writing to each of them, offering his services. Most reply, though this is usually only to say they have no vacancies at the present time. However, one company (one of the big names) asks him to attend an interview.

From a technical standpoint, the interview goes well; the company seems very pleased with Roger's experience and qualifications. The money exceeds Roger's wildest expectations – £29,000 basic and a company car thrown in. But then comes the bombshell: one of the conditions of service is that Commissioning Engineers must be prepared to work anywhere in the EC at 24 hours' notice. Roger baulks. How long will he be away from home? The interviewer shrugs his shoulders and says it depends on the job. Roger explains about his football and how his fiancée won't like the idea of him being away from home for long periods. The interviewer says that in commissioning there's no choice – the work has to be carried out at customers' premises, wherever they happen to be. That is the name of the game.

Roger talks this over with his fiancée. They agree that hardly seeing one another from one week to the next is no basis on which to start a marriage. They decide that Roger should carry on applying for jobs in commissioning, but mention in his letters that he's not prepared to work away.

Roger is looking for a job that probably doesn't exist. If he thought about it long enough, he would realise that commissioning machines has to mean being prepared to work anywhere and everywhere. If he thought about it even further, he would see that the unsociable nature of the job could be one of the reasons the pay is good. Roger's reaction, though, is interesting – he doesn't give up, but instead rewrites the job specification to suit his own situation. He makes up a job that doesn't exist. In effect, he is dictating to the market, or trying to.

Roger is not alone. Countless people are doing the same sort of thing.

- Anne is looking for a job as a Buyer where she can earn £14,000 a year but where she doesn't have to work on Wednesdays (so she can go to college).
- Steve is a Shift Manager looking for a job on days without having to take a drop in salary (he wants to spend more time with his family).
- Richard wants a job in hotel management but doesn't want to work evenings or weekends (he plays in a group).
- Jill is a Sales Rep. She wants a job where she won't have to be in a car on her own after dark (her boyfriend doesn't like the idea).
- Sarah is a newly qualified graduate looking for a job in the computer industry providing it is situated somewhere she can get to on public transport (she doesn't have a car).

These self-imposed limitations effectively wipe out all or most of the available market. But suggesting to people they should think again draws all manner of cries of indignation.

- Anne: 'I want to get a degree. What's unreasonable about that?'
- Steve: 'I don't want my kids growing up and hardly ever seeing me.'
- Richard: 'I can earn £200 a week from gigs. Don't expect me to give it up.'
- Jill: 'What if the car broke down in some dark back street? Do you think it's right a woman should be stuck on her own?'
- Sarah: 'I need money to buy a car. I won't have any money until I get a job.'

The difficulty for Anne and the others arises when they start ignoring the feedback the market gives them because the substance of the feedback is something they don't want to hear. In most cases, they elect to go on pursuing their near-impossible goals. They end up taking their venom out on employers for asking people to do things which are 'unreasonable' or 'unfair'.

Back to our case study, Roger: what should he do? Most importantly, he should take stock of his experiences. They are telling him something. They are telling him the market has no place for Commissioning Engineers who want to stay at home. Then the choices become fairly obvious: either Roger finds ways of tailoring himself to the market, e.g. gives up his football or, along with his fiancée, comes to terms with the fact that he's going to be working away some of the time; or he gives up the Commissioning Engineer idea and looks for jobs which are factory-based.

2.3 Targeting jobs

Having dealt with the pitfalls of applying for jobs you can't do and jobs that don't exist, you now need to be quite clear about exactly the kind of job you are looking for. You need to have some benchmarks or points of reference firmly fixed in your mind. This is known as targeting. Targeting is important. For instance, targeting will help you when you come to start scanning the adverts. It will also help you to brief consultants or anyone else acting on your behalf. Targeting is about being selective. The aim of targeting is twofold:

- it cuts down on time-wasting (notably wasting your time);
- it cuts down on failure ('No thank you' letters and the seeds of discouragement which are inevitably scattered in their wake).

Targeting benchmarks can be changed from time to time, and should be – in the light of experience (our friend flexibility again). Furthermore, there is no reason why you shouldn't have more than one target, i.e. different kinds of job you are going to apply for. This is known as multiple targeting. As we shall see later, multiple targeting has particular benefits for the unemployed.

Targeting benchmarks

The job

This is the easy bit: the job title or kind of work you want to do.

The money

What kind of pay are you looking for? This needs to be related to two factors:

- your present level of earnings;
- the going rate for the kind of job you are targeting (not always easy to establish).

The final figure you arrive at is what is known as your pay expectation.

The hours

For instance, would you be interested in shift-based jobs? If so, there are a number of different patterns to consider. Would you be interested in a job where long hours are the norm? Are you happy to work at weekends or in the evenings, or are you just looking for something part-time? These are all things you need to think through carefully.

The area

Are you looking for work in one particular place, or are you prepared to relocate? Do you have transport? If so, how far are you prepared to travel on a daily basis? If you are relying on public transport, what areas are reasonably accessible by bus or by train from where you live? Do the buses or trains run regularly? If not, you may have to relate this back to your hours-of-work benchmark.

The type of firm

Your qualifications, skills and experience may only lend themselves to particular industries. Under this heading, too, come considerations such as the size of the firm, its attitude to issues such as internal promotion and its prospects for growth. For instance, Marcella, our designer, would only be interested in joining a company where she could expect promotion to a management position within the next two years.

Anything else

Is there anything personal to you which has a bearing on the kind of jobs you can target? For example, you may have a health problem which precludes employment in certain environments, or your domestic circumstances (care of children) may make it impossible for you to entertain a job which entails you being away from home overnight.

> Joseph is a Credit Controller. He works for a firm of electrical wholesalers where he hasn't had a pay rise for over three years. He is earning £13,500 a year and he reckons he's worth at least £18,000.
>
> Up to now Joseph's forays onto the job market have been singularly disappointing. He has written off for a number of jobs and gets interviews without any problem. In most cases, however, the pay turns out to be less than he's earning. Only one company so far has offered more than £14,000 – a catering supplier based on one of the new industrial estates out of town. With the extra bus fares, however, Joseph quickly worked out that he would be £10 a month out of pocket. For this reason he turned down the second interview.
>
> Joseph has noticed how companies never seem to put salaries in advertisements. It seems that you only find out what the pay is when you go along for an interview. Joseph is now getting worried about asking for any more time off work. He thinks his boss is getting suspicious. Taking a tip from a friend, he has now gone along to a local staff agency for help. He has told them what he is looking for, but made it clear he would not be interested in anything under £16,000. This was three months ago.
>
> Joseph rings up the agency from time to time. All they tell him is they have nothing suitable.

Joseph's experiences are an example of targeting going wrong – to the extent that he might even be looking for a job that doesn't exist (the condition we have already described). His pay benchmark is based on nothing more than a personal estimation of his own worth, which is a common mistake. The market – as reflected in his own interview experience and in the staff agency's apparent lack of success – seems to be suggesting that the going rate for Credit Controllers in the town where he lives may fall considerably short of £16,000.

This case study underlines how targeting needs to be flexible and dynamic if it's going to work. It needs to be capable of change and development in the light of experience. Maybe Joseph needs to tweak his pay expectations down a notch or two – or maybe in market terms he's proved to himself the job he's got isn't so badly paid after all.

An important footnote to Joseph's tale is that if, in the light of his experience, he should decide to drop his pay benchmark to, say, £15,000 then he will need to tell the agency – otherwise they will continue to work to his original instructions. Obvious though it sounds, a lot of people fail to communicate changed ideas and circumstances to agencies who are working for them.

Incidentally, we are not going to sidestep the issue of employers' reluctance to disclose salaries in advertisements and the problems this poses for people like Joseph. We will discuss this more fully in Chapter 3.

Targeting and the unemployed

Unemployed people and people who are about to become unemployed may feel that targeting – being selective about which jobs they apply for – is a luxury they can't afford.

Time-wasting may not be a problem to the unemployed but discouragement is. Indeed, discouragement may be one of the major difficulties of long-term unemployment. It is usually the prelude to giving up.

Targeting is still a worthwhile exercise if you are unemployed. Your benchmarks will be different to those of someone in a job, but you will benefit from giving your job-hunting a sense of direction. Unemployed people will particularly benefit from multiple targeting, i.e. targeting several different types of job. We will touch on this again later.

LESSON 1 The three As: accessibility, availability, application

The job market has changed out of all recognition over the last 10–15 years. This is partly due to the effect of two major recessions and partly due to changes in the way in which companies handle recruitment.

A lot of larger companies (traditional providers of quality employment) suffered very badly in the early-1980s' slump. Some of them were wiped off the map altogether. Others cut back or were broken up. This process repeated itself to some extent in 1989–93. So, in town after town across the UK, the 'big-name' employers of yesteryear have either gone or been diminished. What we tend to be left with is a patchwork quilt of small to medium-sized firms, a lot of them quite new.

Typically, the big companies who were such a dominant feature of the employment scene up to the 1970s dealt with recruitment in a structured way. Most of them had a Personnel Department to receive applications and screen candidates. Those who came up to scratch would be put forward to the appropriate manager for final selection.

Most of the small to medium-sized outfits who make up much of today's market don't carry dedicated personnel departments, and as a consequence recruitment is handled in an infinite variety of ways. In most cases, departmental heads or managers do their own recruiting, and what happens will depend on two things:

- how much time and resource they can give to it (bearing in mind they will have other functions to carry out as well);
- how experienced they are.

At its worst, recruitment these days can and does descend into the shambolic. It certainly does not follow, for instance, that a company which is the very model of excellence (in terms of its products or services) will be any good when it comes to recruiting.

Something candidates find particularly hard to cope with is companies who don't bother to reply to their applications. Judging by the number of complaints we hear (there were almost none 15 years ago) not replying seems to be on the increase. Candidates, quite naturally, take this as a slight, an exhibition of the company's disdain for people and general rudeness. Not that we wish to excuse companies who don't reply to candidates' letters, but in most cases behind the scenes is some harassed manager, faced with a key member of staff leaving, who slaps an ad in the local evening paper only to find he's inundated with replies. The chances are he's not used to this situation. He proceeds by picking out a few letters which catch his eye and putting the rest to one side, with the intention of dealing with them later. Another crisis crops up, and another, and the pile of unanswered letters gets shunted from desk to drawer or into filing cabinet, and effectively forgotten.

What this is illustrating is not an upsurge in bad manners but the very changed circumstances in which most managers in business are having to operate. Everything is so much more slimline now. Costs need to be watched. The numbers of administrative staff need to be kept down to the bare minimum. So, not only will today's typical manager have to do without a personnel department, but there won't be an army of assistants and secretaries on tap either.

Inevitably, with these sorts of constraints and pressures, managers have to prioritise – to the extent that some things at the bottom of the list don't get done or don't get done as properly as they might. Those of you who are in management will know precisely what we are talking about – and these comments don't just apply to life in small firms. Managers in big companies are often in the same boat. Big companies may still have Personnel Departments, but it is commonplace to discover that these have been 'downsized' for reasons of cost.

To aspire to career power, you need to have a clear understanding of the true nature of this new market with all its variations and flaws. You also need to be able to use this knowledge to your advantage and to appreciate three things.

- The market is highly competitive. The better the job, the stiffer the competition gets.
- It won't be nice to you.
- It won't give you much time.

The object of this lesson is to introduce you to three fundamental principles – the three As – which we will touch on again and again and which, along with a few more fundamental principles, are going to become the infrastructure of your approach to job-hunting. These three principles are accessibility, availability and application.

Accessibility

A prospective employer must be able to understand who you are, what you have done and what you are capable of doing, completely, clearly and in a very compressed period of time. The presentation of your CV will play a key part in your accessibility, as will your ability to put yourself over lucidly and tersely in interviews.

Availability

A prospective employer must be able to get at you. A cynical view of success in the modern market is that it has less to do with suitability for the job than being in the right place at the right time. Being contactable, being there and being able to attend interviews on cue are part and parcel of availability.

Application

Getting a good job can be hard work and there will be plenty of kicks in the teeth. The road to success will be littered with 'No thank you' letters, bad interview experiences, and times when you will feel the world is a horrible, unfair place. On occasions, too, you will need the skin of a rhinoceros. But, to use the words of an old song, you are going to have to pick yourself up, dust yourself down and start all over again! Application is your ability to be able to keep at it without wavering. It means being single-minded, too – putting your job-hunting above everything else.

The extent to which you adhere to the three As will determine how successful you are going to be at getting good jobs.

2.4 Preparing a CV

CVs are part of the paraphernalia of modern employment. You can't get by without one. Even if you already have a CV, please read this section. Your CV may not be up to scratch – in which case you will have to prepare another one.

There are two rules regarding CVs:

- They must be short (around three pages of A4). Long CVs don't get read.

- They must be crystal clear. They must be capable of being read through once quickly without being misunderstood.

A combination of these two things equals good accessibility. A CV has one purpose – to get you interviews. There is no standard format for a CV, but these are our suggestions on what you need to include.

Essential information to put on your CV

Full name
This should appear prominently at the top of the first page and again on any continuation sheets (just in case your CV should come apart). Continuation sheets need to be numbered too, for the same reason.

Date of birth
People who feel their age may be a disadvantage sometimes leave their date of birth off their CVs. This is an old trick and employers aren't stupid, so don't do it.

Marital status/Children
Single, married, widow(er) or divorced: a simple statement will suffice, e.g. 'Married with two children'.

Address
This should be your home address, including the postcode. Some people (e.g. students and people working away from home) have two addresses. Make it clear which one you want correspondence to be sent to.

Nationality
If you don't have EU nationality, explain your status in the UK and give details of any work permit. Employers will need to know they won't have any hassle if they take you on.

Telephone number

Telephone contactability is an important part of your availability. We know plenty of cases of people who have not been included on interview lists simply because they don't happen to be on the phone; unfair maybe, but in recruitment today that's the way it is.

The hope is that a prospective employer suitably impressed by your CV will pick up the phone and ring you to ask you to come in for an interview. Of course the idea rebounds if you aren't at home and if there is no one else to answer the phone. This is why you need to include alongside your phone number a rough idea of the times you are in (e.g. after 6.30 pm).

You would think that unemployed people are at an enormous advantage in terms of daytime telephone contactability, but even they have to go out from time to time. Hence an idea for unemployed people (to save them sitting by the phone all day waiting for it to ring) is to give time slots for telephone contact (e.g. 'On weekdays I can be contacted on this number between 8 am and 10.30 am or any time after 4 pm'). Having given contact time slots you must stick to them: be there, be disciplined about it – even if the weather's just right for a day's fishing. Absolute application is called for with this.

Telephone answering machines are relatively inexpensive. If you have an answering machine you can advertise the fact on your CV. Recruiters, we find, are quite happy to leave 'Please give me a ring as soon as you can' messages on answering machines.

You may be lucky enough to be in a position where you can be contacted by phone at work or on a mobile. If so, you can enhance your availability even further by giving a daytime contact number. But don't leave yourself open to embarrassing situations. The last thing you want is the boss finding out you are looking for another job; receiving mysterious phone calls at work, especially from companies, can quite easily give the game away. Remember your first duty is to look after the job you've got.

Medical history

Give details of any serious illnesses or operations you have had with the dates. Use plain English rather than medical terms. Avoid the trivial: no one will be interested in the dose of mumps you had when you were 11. If you have no relevant medical history, then say so (don't just miss it out). By your omission an employer may think you are trying to hide something. If you don't smoke, make sure you put this on your CV (there is more on the subject of smoking in section 2.5 below).

Driving licence

State if you have a clean driving licence. If you have some endorsements, give details and the dates when you got them.

Language skills

If you speak any foreign languages, indicate your level of proficiency, e.g. fluent, schoolboy/girl, etc.

Personal statement

This needs to be given some prominence (bold letters or put in a border). The aim is to give the one-time reader in a hurry a quick fix on:

- who you are and what you have done;
- your key strengths;
- what you are looking for (your targets).

What you say needs to be succinct and crystal clear (accessible). Avoid self-eulogies. People who read CVs have seen it all before and won't be impressed.

Pay

Give details of your current salary including any significant perks (such as company car, medical plan, etc.). Also indicate what you are looking for (your pay expectation). The idea here is to cut down on time-wasting. Employers who see that you are after more than they can pay won't take your application any further, so the situation Joseph found himself in shouldn't arise.

If you are unemployed, give details of your earnings in your last job. Like employed people, indicate too what you are looking for.

Simple statements may suffice, such as: 'My salary in my last position was £18,300 p.a. I am trying to maintain the same kind of earnings level.'

Education
List the schools and colleges you attended, with the dates you were there.

Qualifications
List your qualifications, with the dates when you passed the examinations. Also list any current courses of study you are undertaking.

Membership of professional institutions
If you are a member of any professional body connected to your occupation, give details including your grade of membership.

Training courses
List out any training courses you have attended (relevant to your occupation), with the dates and the name of the course organiser.

Employment history
List all the positions you have held. In each case give the name of the company, a brief description of what the company does, your job title, a brief summary of your duties and responsibilities, plus your reason for leaving. Remember something like 'Career advancement' is going to sound better than 'Couldn't get on with the General Manager'. If you are currently unemployed, say so.

Period of notice
Prospective employers will want to know how quickly you can join them. If you are unemployed you can say that you can start immediately.

Leisure activities
Keep this short and simple. People with big long lists of hobbies don't give the impression of being very work-oriented. If you've got any strange hobbies, leave them out.

References

Give the names and addresses and daytime telephone numbers of two referees. Ideally one of these referees will have first-hand knowledge of your work (e.g. an ex-boss); the other will be someone who knows you personally and who will vouch for your character. Get permission before you nominate anyone as a referee (this is important).

Availability for interviews

Put in some statement to the effect that you are available to attend interviews at 'x' days' notice (four or five would seem reasonable – however long it takes to put in a holiday slip) or 'any time' if you are unemployed. We have quite a lot to say about availability for interviews later on.

Typing your CV

Your CV must be typed neatly on plain white A4 paper – never handwritten. Ownership of, or access to, a word-processor or a PC with word-processing software and a good printer is an enormous asset when it comes to preparing a CV. Not only will your finished CV look good but you will also have built-in flexibility, by which we mean:

- you will be able to edit your CV on screen before you print it;
- you will be able to store it on disk for future usage;
- you will be able to chop and change it when you feel like it, or when your circumstances change.

Your software will probably have a spell-checker to stop you making any of those spelling errors employers like to pick up on. A warning, though, about spell-checkers: don't rely on them. With some software Americanisms can creep in, and a spell-checker won't tell you, either, if you've given a proper word the wrong meaning. If your English leaves a bit to be desired, get someone with a good command of spelling and grammar to read through a draft of your CV before you use it. Needless to say, bad spelling and the wrong use of words won't do a lot for you on the first-impressions front.

Second best to a word-processed CV is one prepared on a good modern typewriter by a competent typist – which may of course be you. If not, you may be able to enlist the help of someone in the family, or from among your circle of friends, who has secretarial skills.

A newish powered (electric) typewriter will usually have a decent-enough printer (e.g. a daisywheel) capable of turning out work of a good finished appearance. Old-fashioned manual typewriters are best avoided. Their typefaces are not up to modern standards and uneven finger pressures produce uneven characters – showing just how good old-fashioned typists had to be!

Using a typewriter means you will be typing straight onto the paper as opposed to seeing your typing displayed on a screen. You don't therefore have the facility to edit your text or insert bits you have missed out. Corrections are a problem, too. Your typewriter may come equipped with a lift-off correcting ribbon which enables you to take out words or characters, although there will be a limit as to how far you can 'go back'. Needless to say, rubbings-out or big blobs of correcting fluid should be avoided on a document which is supposed to reflect your character. If you get in a mess, start again.

CVs should be typed in black on plain white, standard-weight, A4 paper. This is not merely a point of style. You may need to photocopy or fax your CV. Coloured print or paper doesn't photocopy or fax very satisfactorily. Flimsy paper or paper which is too thick (people sometimes have CVs typed on card) can be difficult to put through a fax machine. Odd-sized paper may, again, be difficult to put through a fax machine.

Type on one side of the paper only. Typing on the reverse side of a sheet can show up on photocopies and make them look messy.

If you don't have access to a word-processor, you may be tempted to try a commercial word-processing service. You will find any number of these listed in your local telephone and business directories. Another alternative, usually a bit cheaper, is to use a secretary working from home for a bit of extra cash. These people frequently advertise their services in the small ads of local newspapers. Many of them actually say that they type CVs. Whether these secretaries working from home have word-processors or not is something you will need to find out. The key question you should ask is whether they have the capacity to save your CV on disk.

What else do you need to watch out for if you are using a commercial word-processing service?

- The cost – ask 'How much?' Some city-centre secretarial services can be pricey. Also find out what you are getting for your money, i.e. is it just an original, or an original plus 20 copies? Don't expect something for nothing, either.

- Explain *exactly* what you want doing. Don't give them any licence to use their own ideas (see what we have to say about professionally prepared CVs later on). Also give them a handwritten draft to work to.

- Ask for a draft. This will give you a chance to change anything that isn't to your liking. Check the spelling, too. None of these people are above the odd mistake!

- Find out what the arrangements are if you want to update your CV at some point in the future. How much will it cost? The majority of secretarial services will either have a standard charge or base it on the length of time the word-processor operator spends on the task.

• WARNING •

With modern software and a good inkjet or laser printer, the PC owner has the capability to produce a really professional-looking CV (some of the ones we have seen are excellent). But beware the temptation (succumbed to by many) to over-indulge in fancy fonts and graphics. Remember it is a CV you are putting together, not an invitation to a floral fête or an evening of heavy metal music. Keep it plain, keep it simple, and you won't go far wrong.

Getting a second opinion

It is a good idea to let someone else have look at your CV before you put it into its final form. In particular, if you happen to know someone who works (or who has worked) in the relevant employment field, you will find their comments very helpful.

Duplicating your CV

One of the advantages of having your CV stored on disk is that you can print off copies as and when you want. Otherwise, photocopying from an original or master is probably the most accessible way of producing good-quality copies. Never photocopy from a photocopy, as the quality will deteriorate, and for this reason always keep your master in a plastic folder or an envelope to stop it getting dog-eared or soiled.

Plenty of places offer photocopying services, from the local library through to specialist high-street print shops. Photocopies aren't expensive. The main consideration for you is the finished appearance. You will want your copies to look clean and crisp, and hard to tell from the original. Poor photocopies (typically greyish-looking and dark round the edges) tend to reflect the equipment (old or poorly maintained) or the operator's skills (or lack of them).

A useful tip is not to have too many copies run off: 20 will probably suffice. Any more and you will find they are out of date before you use them (see what we have to say about updating your CV).

> **LESSON 2** Early impressions
>
> Why go to all this trouble with the appearance of your CV? For a start, it is a reflection of you (which is important enough), but the other point to bear in mind is that a scruffy-looking CV runs the risk of not being read. It doesn't get you interviews, so it fails.
>
> But there is a bigger issue here – early impressions and their importance. Your CV, when you think about it, is the very first impression of you a prospective employer receives. It sends out a signal, and that signal, good or bad, is very hard to shift. This is the thing to remember about early impressions: they stick. In other words, your CV sets the agenda.

Recycled CVs

CVs which have been sent out before are a distinct turn-off. They're easy to spot – typically fingered, scuffed and dog-eared. Apart from the offence factor, they carry the tale of someone who has been round on the job market for some time (i.e. a failure). Copies of your CV should be sent out in pristine condition. They should be viewed as entirely disposable – for one-time use only. If an employer returns your CV, throw it away. Never ask for it back, either. This is another reason for not having CVs which are voluminous or elaborately bound.

Storing your CVs

Don't store your CVs anywhere where they will pick up strong smells. A waft of stale cigarette smoke or burgers as it comes out of the envelope first thing in the morning won't do much for you on the first-impressions front.

Updating your CV

If you are active on the job market, you must keep your CV up to date. If you get some further qualification, or if your personal circumstances change, then you will need to record this information on your CV. Updating your CV can be irksome, particularly if you happen to have 100 copies stored away in the cupboard. This is why we recommended not having too many run off in the first place. Handwriting an addendum or trying to type the new information into a ridiculously small space usually results in a mess. Take our tip – start afresh. You will feel happier if you do. Of course, you won't have this problem if your CV is stored on disk. Updating will be relatively easy.

Another useful tip is to update your CV straight away. Don't wait until you have a need. You'll find that when you want a CV you want it in a hurry.

• WARNING •

Good CV management (updating and having current copies to hand) is strongly recommended, but tweaking and twiddling isn't. Some people are changing their CVs all the time, not because anything substantial has happened to them but because they decide A might look better swapped round with B, or C ought to be given a bit more prominence than D. The home-PC fraternity are particularly culpable in this respect. It may seem harmless enough, until the question of 'Which version of my CV have you got?' arises – usually in the middle of an interview. You have one version (the latest); the interviewer has an earlier attempt (perhaps forwarded by an agency or because the original application was made some time ago). Confusion arises; interview time is lost, and worst of all the interviewer may be left with the lingering suspicion that you are trying to pull the wool over his/her eyes (a very bad early impression).

Avoid constantly trying to gild the lily. If you want to appraise your CV, do it against what counts – its performance. Does your CV get you interviews? If it doesn't, it might need some attention. If it does, leave it alone.

Having your CV professionally prepared

If you feel you can't be bothered to prepare your own CV, you can pay someone to do it for you. People in the market for top jobs (senior management) feel almost obliged to get their CVs put together by an expert. They feel they may be selling themselves short if they don't.

The only investment that is needed to go into the business of CV-preparation is a word-processor. Unfortunately, this means anyone can do it and, for this reason, you need to be careful before you go forking out substantial sums of money for someone to prepare a CV for you. They actually may not be any better qualified at it than you are.

On the whole, CV-preparers tend to fall into two categories. The first group we have already touched on – these are essentially typing/secretarial services or individuals working from home who will have a skeleton CV set up on their word-processor into which they can pump your details. In other words, what they are offering is fairly minimal. Into the second group come a wide assortment of individuals and organisations, usually people claiming some expertise in the employment field. They will do you a super-swish, tailor-made CV and spend time with you deciding what should go in it. One of the main differences between these two groups is the price. Bespoke CVs can be very expensive and it pays (always) to find out how much it is going to cost before you proceed.

We have mixed feelings about professionally prepared CVs. Unfortunately, a lot of them are far too long, and for this reason alone fail the accessibility test. But perhaps the worst feature of a CV that has been prepared by someone else is its lack of 'personality'. Homespun CVs, for all their rough edges, always contain something of the candidate – the way they express themselves, the words they choose, how they view themselves – there is something for the reader to identify with and to latch onto. The all-important engagement factor starts to work: 'Here is a candidate I feel I know' translates into 'Here is a candidate I want to interview'. The CV, in other words, does its job. In contrast, there is something clinical and sanitised about professionally prepared CVs. The standard descriptions and superlatives could be about almost anyone. The candidate, sadly, just doesn't come through, and such CVs become boring and predictable to read. In some cases, it is possible to recognise who the preparer is. Perversely, something that is intended to create good early impressions can do the exact reverse.

So do have a shot at preparing your own CV. Apart from saving yourself a bit of cash, you may be quite pleased with the result.

Two CVs

Some candidates' skills and experiences clearly qualify them for more than one type of job or career. For example, the Chartered Accountant who has run a business might feel equally at home in the accountancy profession or in a general management position. Encapsulating these widely differing suitabilities and ambitions in a single CV might prove difficult (bearing in mind the need to confine CVs to short, sharp messages). One way round the problem is to have two CVs (why not more, indeed?). But, if you do this, you must always record which CV you have sent to which employer.

2.5 Preparing yourself

You now have an accessible CV and you are aware of the pitfalls of applying for jobs that don't exist or jobs you can't do. You have also done your targeting. What else do you need to do before you put yourself onto the market?

Time off work

Applying for jobs means attending interviews. Unless you are unemployed, attending interviews means having time off work, and having time off work means problems for you. Not many employers will do interviews out-of-hours, and it is no use banking on this. Finding you can't go to interviews because you can't get time off work effectively means you're wasting your time applying in the first place. This is yet another illustration of the importance of availability. You should remember, too, that many jobs (especially the good ones) will require two or even three interviews (sometimes more).

Stock excuses, like going to the dentist's or feeling poorly, soon start to wear thin, and you should remember in all of this that your first duty is to protect the job you've got. So don't, whatever you do, find yourself in hot water with the boss because of the amount of time you're taking off work.

Itinerants – people like salesmen – may be able to squeeze in interviews 'between calls'. Managers and professionals don't, on the whole, get quizzed too closely on their comings and goings. Part-timers and people who work shifts are possibly best placed, but for the rest of us keeping back a few days' floating holiday is usually all we can manage. It will help you of course if you can take holidays in half-days. But to give yourself sufficient floating holidays it may be necessary for you to consider abandoning some of your plans for holiday away – not to your liking, perhaps, but remember what we had to say about the need for application and putting your job-hunting first.

The greatest difficulty arises for those people who have to have fixed holidays (e.g. shutdowns). Often they are left with no choice other than making awkward excuses or asking for time off for 'personal reasons'.

Whatever your circumstances, if you are working then the amount of time you have available for interviews is limited. This is why you must treat it as precious and not to be squandered.

Planning your holidays

This is another availability issue. If you are away on holiday, prospective employers won't be able to contact you. You won't be able to attend interviews either. There is obviously a point of conflict here, the only answer to which lies in compromise. Try to avoid long holidays when you are job-seeking. Holidays of more than two weeks are definitely out. If you break your holidays up into one-week periods, then so much the better. Remember, too, the point we made about keeping back a few days' floating holiday for interviews.

We frequently get unemployed people quite desperate for work but who, sensing 'nothing's happening', take themselves off for long and open-ended periods in tents or caravans, or go to holiday homes where they can't be contacted. The message is – don't; not unless there is someone at home to answer the phone and open the post. Be sure, too, that you can be reached; if necessary, ring in every couple of days. Always be prepared to come scuttling back if you have to.

Carrying out an availability audit

This is an interesting exercise. How available are you? Put yourself in the position of a prospective employer trying to get hold of you.

Just how easy is it? You've given your home telephone number in your CV. You have said you are normally in after 6.30 pm. Now put it to the test over, say, a two-week period. Prospective employers will take you very literally. 'After 6.30 pm' means 6.31 pm. If they fail to get through, they may try again ten minutes later. So monitor what would happen if someone tried to phone you at 6.31 pm and 6.41 pm, on the dot, each evening, Monday to Friday. Would you be in? Would anyone be in? Would another person know what to do? Most importantly, how many times would the number be engaged?

The purpose of this exercise is to expose the flaws in your availability – flaws which will probably surprise you, such as:

- how often you are late;
- how often you tend to pick up the phone the minute you walk through the door, thereby frustrating any one trying to contact you;
- how long members of your family spend chatting on the phone and hogging the line (especially early in the evening);
- how many times the phone is answered by children who, unless they're coached differently, might greet callers with 'Sorry, there's no one in'.

An availability audit is intended to throw up some points for action. Included in these points might be the need to introduce some disciplines at home, e.g. a golden rule about not using the phone between 6.30 and 7 pm, or schooling everyone on how to deal properly with important callers. A word of warning is that unavailability can sometimes have unusual causes. We know one gentleman whose dog was in the habit of pulling the phone plug out of the socket. Answer: keep the dog out of the hall.

Availability is important to you in this instantaneous world of modern employment. We warned you that employers won't be prepared to spend time on you. If they find you hard to get hold of, they will simply give you a miss and move on to someone else. This is the risk.

Editing your answering machine

Not everyone is in the habit of putting silly messages on their answering machines, but some people do and some of the messages verge on the imbecilic and irritating. Worse still, some might even be classified as offensive. No doubt the perpetrators of these messages find them extremely funny (why else do they do it?) and, to be fair, they probably intend them solely for the amusement of their family and friends. The simple point is this: if you are the owner of an answering machine it's a good availability tool, but be sure the message on it is something you would be happy for a prospective employer to hear. If in doubt, wipe it out – before you start sending off CVs. Remember what we said in Lesson 2 about early impressions. If your CV is your first impression, your answering machine might be your second. Good or bad, these early impressions stick and rarely shift. The normal 'We're sorry we're not in at the moment, but if you would like to leave your name and number after the tone we'll get back to you as soon as we can' is probably the safest bet.

Also get into the habit of checking your answering machine when you walk in – if you don't do this already. And do remember to switch it on!

Brushing up your telephone answering

Once your CV has gone out, there is the possibility that prospective employers will ring you at home – at least that's what we're hoping for. Good early impressions are at stake here, so polish up your telephone answering manner. This needn't be anything fancy. A simple 'John Smith, good evening' will do nicely – crisp, polite ... and learn to sound cheerful too! No one wants a 'misery guts'.

At the same time as polishing up your own telephone answering, you might brief members of your household to do the same. The sort of gutteral one-worders much loved by teenagers won't do you a lot of good.

Trying to conduct a telephone conversation over a barrage of noise is irritating enough for both parties; but having to ask a caller to hold while you yell at someone to turn the telly down or shut the kids up or take the barking dog outside is the stuff of embarrassment. It is hard to get your aplomb back afterwards.

Giving up smoking

Attitudes towards smokers have hardened a lot in the last 10–15 years, so much so that anti-smoker discrimination is now rife in employment and people who smoke need to focus on this fact. We appreciate that giving up smoking isn't easy but, if you can, it will greatly enhance your job prospects. 'Do you smoke?' is a question increasingly being asked at interviews.

Summary

One of the sad features of today's market is the large number of people thrashing round in it with poorly thought-out ideas on what they are doing or where they are going. Without knowing it, many of these people are chasing false hopes: jobs they can't do; jobs that don't exist. Others, meanwhile, are applying for anything and everything. Both groups combined make up what to employers is the time-waster element: the candidates who don't stand a chance, candidates who automatically get turned down.

Perhaps the saddest fact of all is that many of these people are doing what they are doing out of a sense of desperation – feeling they have no other options. Frequently they are people who have been out of work a long time and who think they have 'tried everything'. They end up discouraged, and that's no good at all.

The first thing we have attempted to do in this chapter is to encourage you to get some form, some sense of direction into your job-seeking. We have done this in three ways.

- Restraining you in your pursuit of difficult or unobtainable objectives. In doing this, we would not want to thwart you in some of your bigger ambitions but instead get you to see that some applications are highly speculative – the odds are stacked against you from the start because other candidates have more experience and these days employers play safe. This is particularly the case where you are trying to take big leaps up the ladder, or where you are trying to change careers. Carrying on is OK providing you realise your chances are slim and the most likely outcome is 'No'.

- Getting you to define your targets properly and to think these through. We want you to do this formally, because in the next chapter we will be using your targets as the basis for deciding which jobs you should be applying for and conversely which you should be leaving alone.

- Getting you to learn from your experiences; to listen to the messages you get back from the market and to use this information for your fine-tuning.

The modern market is something you have got to learn to live with. It is not a tidy place. If you want to go out and get yourself a good job, compare it to taking a shopping trip round a maze of little sidestreets. Some of the shops you come across will be big; some of them will be small; some will have big snazzy windows, while others will be poked up tiny little back alleys where you will hardly notice them. Before you set off on this shopping trip it is clearly going to pay you to know which shop sells what. It is also going to pay you to know what you want to buy. Otherwise you will waste a lot of your time wandering round not accomplishing very much except standing at the back of long queues and finding at the end of the day that all the best bargains have gone.

The modern job market is a bit like this. Some employers are very adept at recruiting (the big snazzy windows where all the goods are clearly on display) but the rest, the vast majority, aren't. You have to learn to poke around a bit to unearth the best buys. Often you will have to ask the shopkeeper what he's got under the counter. Sometimes he'll be out the back doing something else, so you will have to ring the bell a few times.

To enable you to articulate yourself towards the right goals in this difficult and unreceptive market we have introduced you to three principles: accessibility, availability and application – the three As. Simple though they are, the three As provide the underpinning to productive job-hunting in today's tough market.

If we take a structured view of getting good jobs, your first task is to get yourself interviews. This isn't always easy. Where the job has been advertised and where you will be one of many applicants, getting an interview could prove decidedly difficult.

As part of putting yourself on the market you will need a really effective CV. A CV is there to do the business for you and to get you interviews. Where the competition for a job is intense, being 'suitable' doesn't necessarily guarantee you an interview. For a start, a prospective employer has got to be able to see that you are suitable, which means your suitability has got to come across in one quick read of your CV. Your CV, in other words, has to be accessible. It has got to deliver the message for you clearly.

The other factor in the getting-you-to-the-interview equation is that the prospective employer must be able to get hold of you with a minimum of fuss and messing round. This is your availability, and your availability has got to be given a great deal of prominence in your CV. For the purposes of your appreciation of availability, assume that the employer you are trying to get the interview with is some poor overworked senior manager with more than enough to do and no help to hand (sounds familiar?). In deciding who to ask along for an interview, someone like this will be drawn to a candidate who can offer one-phone-call contactability. The reverse applies to candidates who can't. Interview lists are frequently decided on points like these.

The presentation of your CV, its appearance, is also of vital importance. The first impression an employer forms of you as a candidate will be based on your CV. The importance of early impressions has been stressed – early impressions stick. In Chapter 3 you will be learning about halo effects. Halo effects sum up the situation where some quite glaring flaw in a candidate gets overlooked (particularly at an interview) because the candidate has made favourable first impressions. The concern employers have about halo effects demonstrates just how powerful good early impressions can be. Conversely, a bad early impression (e.g. a scruffy CV) will be hard to dispel.

We hope you will succeed in getting interviews, but if you do while you are in employment you will find you are going to need time off work to attend. We have encouraged you to view your time-off-work time as precious and not to be squandered. In particular, you must not squander your time-off-work time on interviews for jobs which don't match up to your targeting benchmarks. If you can't get any more time off without creating problems for yourself, your all-important availability is gone.

Also, regarding availability, you need to check out that your telephone contactability works and that you can be contacted where and when you say you can be contacted on your CV. Modern employers won't waste time on you – if your phone's always engaged or if you never seem to be in they will give you a miss. They will move on to someone else, and in competitive situations (good jobs, which have been advertised) there will be plenty of 'someone elses' waiting to take your place.

Questions and answers

Leaving jobs off your CV

Q *I worked for one company for over 20 years but recently I have had a lot of jobs. Frankly I found it hard to settle after so long with one firm. I know this won't look good on my CV, so should I leave some of the jobs out?*

A Not settling after a long period of employment with one company is a well-known phenomenon – in other words, what has happened to you is not as unusual as you think. However, the trouble with what you are proposing is that any jobs you get offered will be on the basis of untrue information you have given about yourself. If an employer finds out at some point in the future that the information on your CV is incorrect, then, technically speaking, he is entitled to dismiss you. Whether he would do this or not is another question, particularly if you happen to have proved yourself in the job by then. On the whole, we think you would be happier without the feeling that there might be an axe dangling over your neck. So list out your succession of jobs.

Employers, particularly the better ones, don't expect people to be perfect, but they do expect them to be honest. A little footnote at the end of your CV to explain the difficulties you have had may be a help too.

Is a long period of notice an off-putter?

Q *My period of notice is three months. If I put this in my CV, won't it put people off?*

A Three months is by no means unusual these days, especially if you are in a position of responsibility. The putting-off can in fact work in reverse, e.g. if a senior manager says in his CV that he only has to give a week's notice this arouses suspicion straight away. It is true, however, that long periods of notice won't appeal to companies in a hurry. The word 'negotiable' in brackets after the period of notice might help soften the blow. At the end of the day, though, facts are facts – don't start making statements in your CV like 'My period of notice is three months but I am prepared to give less'. This puts you in a shabby light.

Asking too little

Q *From talking to friends who do similar jobs I have come to the conclusion that I am very underpaid. This does not surprise me because the Building Society I work for has a reputation for being parsimonious with its staff. If I write off for other jobs and state my present salary I am worried that employers will take advantage of me, i.e. offer me less than they would pay someone who is earning a decent rate. Friends have suggested I re-do my CV and put a couple of thousand on my salary. But don't I run the risk of being found out? A new employer would only have to look at my P45 to see I hadn't told the truth.*

A Yes, you are quite right – a new employer will be able to see what you have earned so far in the tax year by looking at your P45. Whether this would alter the employer's view of you is a different question.

Your problem raises a number of points about pay targeting – notably that as well as putting your present pay in your CV and letters of application you should also state what you are looking for. Let us assume for the sake of argument that your only reason for going out on the market is pay, i.e. your present job is secure and you have no other significant grouses. Let us assume also that you are being paid £15,000 a year for whatever it is you do. Finally, let us assume that your friends are telling you that £20,000 is the going rate. We have no quarrel with you for listening to friends. Because pay is such a secretive business, anecdotal information is often as good as you get (at least until you start building up your own bank of experience).

In setting pay-targeting benchmarks, two items come into play – your present earnings and the elusive market rate. People who feel they are underpaid are acknowledging that there is a huge disparity between the two (in other circumstances this wouldn't be the case) What you need to do is to set out your stall in your CV and any letters of application, i.e. say that you are being paid £15,000 now but that you are looking for £20,000 (no less). This will have the effect of stopping short any employer who thinks you can be got on the cheap. Stick to your guns, at least up to the point where your experience on the market starts to suggest to you £20,000 is asking too much (if it ever does). You are quite right to have this fear of being ripped off. But don't indulge in worrying deceptions to prevent it from happening. Proceed in a straightforward way by making it clear to the world that just because you are underpaid now doesn't mean you want to go on being underpaid. Stating pay expectations clearly is especially important for someone in your position.

Targeting difficult – not sure what you are looking for

Q *I am a 23-year-old business studies graduate. I left university 18 months ago and took a job in sales. This was a disaster. I was not good at it and in the end I failed: I got the sack. Frankly, I haven't got the faintest idea what to do now. Some people have suggested I go back to college to get further qualifications; others urged me to try something less pressurised, such as computer work or accounts. Going back to college is out of the question because I don't have the finance – neither does there seem to be much point. But how is someone like me supposed to go about targeting? Even I don't know what I want.*

A The general idea behind targeting is to get some structure into your applications. Thrashing round aimlessly in the job market will do you no good at all. The biggest risk you run is ending up feeling disappointed and discouraged – in your case feeling that all the hard work and study that went into getting your degree was for nothing. This will be the result if you start applying for anything and everything, then finding you get turned down because you haven't got the experience required. First things first. Feel positive: you are young and quite clearly very capable but, in your initial choice of career, you made a mistake. Everyone is entitled to make one mistake, especially with their first job. Even two or three mistakes don't matter. The important thing you have learned from this mistake is that you are no good at sales. You may have learned a few things about yourself at the same time. Most of all, see your position as one of opportunity.

Now move on to your targeting. Remember there is nothing wrong with having more than one target. Start with jobs in data processing if you like. Get an idea of where fresh graduates slot in and start drawing up your targeting benchmarks from there. Sources of information might be: people you know in data processing (friends, family, people who were with you at university); lecturers; or employment agencies who specialise in DP staff. You will be surprised what you can put together in a few hours' research. (This approach contrasts with picking up the paper every Thursday, scanning the ads and thinking 'I'll write off for this, this and that' because 'this, this and that' happen to be there and they are all jobs you think you can do.)

THREE

MAKING APPLICATIONS

Having prepared you for venturing out onto the modern job market, we are now going to look at how to find out about good jobs and how to go about applying for them.

3.1 Finding out about jobs

Rumour has it that the best jobs are never advertised. Is this true? In this chapter, we will look at the various ways in which you can 'source the market', including the 'invisible market'.

Cold calling

This means phoning firms up to see if they have anything for you. Done properly, cold calling can be used to very good effect. A cold call yields a snapshot picture. The information you get will be correct for just a short period of time. Expect nothing more from your cold calls and you won't be disappointed.

The mistake – and plenty of people make it – is cold calling a target just once and leaving your name and address or sending in a copy of your CV. Your name and address gets scribbled on a piece of paper. Your CV gets put on the pile (every manager has a pile of unsolicited CVs on the desk). Frankly, the likelihood of either seeing the light of day again is extremely remote.

Getting results from cold calling comes from being persistent and methodical (another illustration of application). Here is what you need to do.

- Do your homework. Target the right companies – companies that are likely to have the kind of vacancies you are looking for. You will know some likely targets already. Local trade directories can be very useful sources. So too are the job ads in the papers. They often give information about companies and what they do – even if the jobs being advertised are outside your field. From job ads you can also tell which companies are recruiting.

- Avoid making calls when key people in companies are likely to be busy. First thing in the morning and last thing at night are bad times. Fridays are never very good either, for the same reasons. Companies' lunch breaks vary: it's best not to try between 12 noon and 2pm. Keeping to 10am to 12 noon and 2–4pm on Mondays to Thursdays will minimise unproductive time.

- Be direct with telephonists and tap into their knowledge. Say you are looking for a job in such-and-such a field, and ask who would be the best person to speak to. Avoid jargon and use terminology telephonists will understand.

- Get names. This is particularly important if the person you need to speak to is unavailable and you will have to ring back. When you do, you won't have to go through the same preamble with the telephonist. You can ask for the person you want straight away.

- When you get connected to the right person, sound fresh. Unless you are in telesales and used to it, you will tend to feel jaded after long bouts of cold calling, and this will tell in your voice. One way to avoid sounding stale is to take breaks every now and then. A change of activity, like making a cup of coffee, will help.

- Stop the minute you start to feel fed up.

- If your call has struck lucky and the company has the kind of vacancy you are looking for, then find out what you have to do to apply.

- If there's nothing doing, then do your bit of market research and find out if the company ever has vacancies of the type you require. Keep this brief. The person you are talking to will be busy and facing a quizzing from an unsolicited caller can become annoying. End the call by saying 'Thank you' and that you will try again another time.

- Keep a record of the calls you make (when you made them, to whom you spoke, and any useful information you gleaned). Don't rely on your memory. After a while, one cold call will blur into another. We have a lot more to say on the subject of keeping records (see page 105).

- Rate your calls on a scale of 0 to 5 according to their potential. For instance, give a score of 5 to firms who drop out strong hints that they could well be interested in someone like you at some point in the future. Firms with less certain needs will probably rate 2 or 3. Zero the no-hopers or people who get shirty with you. Don't give them any more of your precious time.

- Proceed systematically from here on. Keep up regular contact with your 5s. Put them perhaps on a six-week call cycle (more often and you start to run the risk of being viewed as a pest). Your 2s and 3s might be worth ringing every three or four months. Be ready, though, to change your ratings (upwards or downwards). In this way, you will eventually have all your target companies on a call plan. The number of new companies you will be ringing will diminish as time goes on. Incidentally, you may find that a wall-planner is helpful (and it is inexpensive and available from most stationers).

- As you get into your stride with cold calling, you will find that you will be making fewer and fewer calls, but the calls you are making will be increasingly well targeted. In short, the effectiveness of cold calling will improve over a period. This is where you start to get results. Sooner or later you will start to connect with good jobs. Statistical probability takes the place of pure luck.

Dedicated and methodical cold calling can be an excellent way of sourcing jobs – often before they are advertised or put out to recruitment consultants.

Mailshots

Mailing your CV is the literary alternative to cold calling. It is another way of saying 'Here I am, this is what I want and is there anything for me at the moment?', but putting it in writing this time. Unlike cold calling, putting together a mailshot is something you can do at any time. You don't have to do it in office hours and have time off work. You can organise your mailshot in the evening or at weekends. You can mail as many firms as you like for the price of a stamp (and whatever a copy of your CV costs).

So what are the snags? Unfortunately, too many people have jumped on the mailshot bandwagon; this includes a lot of people who just send their CVs off to anyone and everyone – people who employers view as no-hopers and time-wasters. Job clubs for the unemployed, run by Job Centres, even offer facilities to send out mailshots. Saturation of this sort inevitably takes its toll. Unsolicited CVs pile up on managers' desks. Some get read; some don't.

A mailshot has a further drawback. Because it is impersonal, it provides no feedback, no information from which you can learn. Unless you happen to strike lucky, the best you can probably hope for is a standard word-processed acknowledgement thanking you for writing and regretting that there are no suitable vacancies for you at the present time. In most cases, though, you won't receive a reply. Don't get wound up about this. If you do, you're wasting your energy.

Here are a few tips on how to make mailshots work best for you.

- Again, do your homework. Target the right kind of companies.
- Give them a ring before you put anything in the post. The object of this exercise is to get a name. Ideally, the name you want is the name of the person who will have the say-so on hiring people like you. For example, if you are a Sales Manager you will want the name of the Sales Director; if you are an Accountant, you will want the name of the Financial Manager; and so on. Again, tap into that fount of all knowledge: our friend the helpful telephonist. You can explain who you are and what you are trying to do (to overcome any caginess). Don't be fobbed off with the name of the

Personnel Manager. Personnel Managers have got a bigger pile of unsolicited CVs on their desks than anyone else. Sales Directors and Financial Managers won't be quite so inundated. For this reason, your CV will stand a better chance of being read (and being read by the right person).

- Put together a covering letter to go with your CV. Keep this to a brief explanation of why you are writing (the kind of job you are looking for) and how you can be contacted (even though this information is given in your CV). Covering letters look better typed, but handwriting is acceptable providing your handwriting is legible and you use black ink. Use plain white A4 paper (like your CV). Don't get a load of standard letters run off with blank spaces for writing in names and dates. No one likes to feel they are part of a mailshot. It certainly doesn't encourage a response.

- Use plain white A4 envelopes. This saves you having to fold your CV, and it won't arrive at the other end looking like a concertina. (Remember what we said about first impressions being impressions that stick. The first thing the recipient of a folded CV does is try to flatten it out – as a result of which it will no longer be in mint condition.)

- Use first-class post. For a few extra pennies, it creates an aura of importance about what the envelope contains – again, a first-impression point. It is vital to make sure you put the right amount of postage on. Companies rightly feel very displeased about having to pay excess mail charges on unsolicited correspondence (extremely negative first impressions). Standard first-class postage covers you up to 60g.

- Mark your envelope 'Confidential'. This is just another device to ensure that it is opened by the right pair of hands.

- Don't mail too many CVs at the same time. Trickle them out over a period of weeks. This will help avoid the situation where you create more interest than you can cope with, i.e. you get invited to more interviews than you can attend because of the constraints on your available time off work. Obviously this consideration doesn't apply if you are unemployed.

- Don't bother to follow up on mailshots by ringing in after a few days to find out if the CV has been received. In our view, this is scratching twice on the same patch. Apart from the odd bit of feedback, the effort is better put into cold calling.

After you have done a batch of mailshots, stop and take stock. What result have you had? Unfortunately with mailshots it is very difficult to quantify success. A lot depends on your marketability. For instance, you would expect that a 35-year-old, time-served Engineer to attract more interest than a 58-year-old former Bank Manager with a health problem, and this clearly needs to be taken into account. However, the point of getting you to review the performance of your mailshots from time to time is to stop you carrying on regardless of any lessons that you may have learned. Failing to do this inevitably sets you on the fatal road to discouragement and unnecessarily giving up. Absence of feedback, as we have noted, is one of the big drawbacks of mailshots. Usually, you are left to form your own conclusions, which can of course be completely wrong.

If you are getting absolutely no response to mailshots, except for the odd standard acknowledgement, this checklist may help you identify where the problem lies.

- Revisit your CV and maybe get some second opinions. Leave your CV alone if the flaws you pick up are only minor ones.
- Re-examine your targeting. Are you guilty of mailing anyone and everyone?
- Carry out an availability audit (see page 61). Could it be that you're not available when employers are trying to call you?

Faxshots

Home fax machine ownership has given an important new dimension to job sourcing. Faxes, on the whole, are read – often within minutes of transmission. There is the added bonus that people tend to react to faxes and react quickly. This, however, does not alter the fact that, in order to work, a faxshot still has to hit the target at the right time. There still has to be a need within the organisation which the recipient sees as matching your skills, qualifications and experience.

Are there any drawbacks to faxshots? Three are worthy of mention.

- As with mailshots, there is an absence of feedback.
- Fax paper is crinkly and dog-ears easily. A faxed CV soon starts to look tatty. The fact that faxes fade over a period of time doesn't matter too much. Faxshots have only got a limited life.
- Faxes are not very confidential. Companies' fax machines are often situated in general offices, and incoming faxes can be read by anyone who happens to be around. Bearing in mind that your CV contains information on your present employment and details of your salary, you may not find this very acceptable. This is less of a problem of course for the unemployed.

Treat faxshots rather like mailshots. Start by finding out the name of the right person to whom to send your fax. Here are some other points to bear in mind for getting the best results.

- Do a lead sheet. This lead sheet serves the same purpose as an accompanying letter. Apart from explaining why you are faxing your CV, your lead sheet will say how many sheets you are sending (just in case any don't go through). It will also tell the other end what to do if your fax is incomplete, i.e. ring you immediately. Also give a phone number on which you can be contacted over the following few hours (a good bit of instant availability for you here).
- At the same time that you are finding out the name of the right person to send your fax to, you can enquire if there is a confidential fax line you can use.
- Send faxes during normal working hours and not too late in the afternoon. Faxes left lying around overnight have a habit of going missing.
- Send faxshots one at a time or in small batches well spaced apart. As with mailshots, this will help avoid the situation where you get more leads than you can cope with.

- Number your sheets so they can be easily pinned together when they reach the other end.
- Carry out the same periodic review procedures as with mailshots.

The opportunity to use a fax machine is yet another reason for you having a CV that is not too long. One of the 25-pagers we occasionally get a sight of would take ages to go through a fax machine. The company whose fax line you are jamming up won't be overpleased, and you can bet that the machine will run out of paper when you are halfway through transmitting.

Professional networking

This means using your contacts to source jobs for you. If you work in a commercial undertaking, your professional network often extends to customers and suppliers – and, more importantly in this context, competitors. Two other professional networks worth mentioning are:

- professional institutions: try attending local branch meetings and getting to know other people in your line of work;
- ex-colleagues – people you once worked with who have moved on.

There is no great mystique to professional networks. Everyone has them. They are a natural consequence of being in a career. Using your professional networks to source jobs for you involves little more than putting a word in the right ear, or making the odd discreet phone call; but there are a few drawbacks.

- People in careers live in a tight-knit world. Word you're on the look-out for another job can get fed back to the wrong quarters (e.g. your boss). You need to be careful about whom you speak to.
- Networking within the same trade can bring you into conflict with contractual restraints. There may be something in your terms of employment which says you can't work for a competitor.
- You will only ever source a narrow slice of the market. It is important, therefore, that you use other sourcing methods alongside professional networking.

A final point about professional networks is that they spawn two-way traffic. Information about jobs can get fed to you without you having to provide a stimulus. This brings us on to our next method of sourcing – approach.

Approach

The use of approach as a means of recruiting staff has flourished in recent years. Firms see two advantages to using approach:

- either directly, or indirectly via a consultant, they have foreknowledge of the person being approached – this lessens the risks in external recruitment;
- it shortcuts the need for lengthy selection procedures.

Approaches are sometimes made by search consultants (headhunters), and sometimes by firms themselves.

Approach makes up a sizeable part of the 'invisible' market, and this begs the question: what can you do to enhance your chances of being approached? On the face of it, approach is an event you have no control over. It comes to you out of the blue, or so it seems. Yet in reality a lot of approach is stimulated by professional networking. A vacancy arises and someone (an ex-colleague or a trade contact, perhaps) brings your name up.

How do you get yourself noticed by professional head-hunters? If you make a habit of reading the recruitment pages of the press, you will notice that a lot of these firms style themselves as 'selection and search consultants'; this means they do standard selection assignments as well as head-hunting. So if you apply for a job advertised by a firm of selection consultants there's a reasonable chance that you'll be introducing yourself to people who do head-hunting as well. A copy of your CV will end up on their files. This is the key.

Job Centres

You will find a Job Centre in practically every high street in the UK. You can walk in and view the cards on display. These cards give details of current vacancies and are arranged in categories. If anything catches your eye, you can make enquiries at the counter.

Job Centres are a public service. They make no charges to either candidates or employers. Job Centres have come in for a bit of criticism over the years, not least from employers. From the job-seeker's point of view, the biggest problems with Job Centres are as follows.

- Not all the vacancies on display are current. This is not necessarily the Job Centre's fault. Employers will fill vacancies and not tell them.

- There is a general feeling among employers that Job Centres don't perform very well in providing candidates for jobs which call for any degree of qualification, skill or experience. In consequence, better jobs don't tend to get notified to Job Centres; employers go for other methods of recruitment instead. Describing Job Centres as sources of low-skill, low-paid, casual or part-time employment is going a bit too far, but it is true to say that unless you're looking for work in the public sector good career jobs don't tend to feature very strongly on the noticeboards in the Job Centre.

- Job Centre opening times coincide with the times that most people are at work.

Employment agencies/consultants

The one hard fact about employment agencies and firms of recruitment consultants is that there are enough of them. If taken collectively, they are an important source of jobs and a way of tapping into the part of the market that is not advertised (the invisible market). They are also an important (vital) source of complementary-sector, short-term work (more on this in Chapter 6). Registering with an agency is relatively simple. It usually involves paying a visit and filling in a form. Agencies make their money from employers, not from you; so as far as you are concerned their services come free. Once an agency has you on file it will use its knowhow and connections to find you what you want.

Many agencies are open 'out of hours', or they will have late-opening evenings, so that people wishing to register with them won't have to have time off work.

It is important that you choose the right agency (or agencies). A quick glance in your local directory under 'Employment Agencies' will show you just how many there are in your area. If you live in a city or an industrial area, the list will run into hundreds. So just how do you go about selecting a suitable agency? Where do you start? The agency you choose must be capable of sourcing suitable jobs in your target area. It must, therefore, meet the following two criteria.

- It must handle the kind of appointments you are targeting. For example, if you are looking for a position in financial management it is absolutely pointless registering with an agency whose strength lies in the technical field.
- Its catchment area must cover the area you are targeting. Some agencies are quite small and only operate within a defined locality.

Begin your search for the best agency by going though all your local directories (look under 'Employment Agencies'). Employment agencies come and go, so make sure you are using current directories – not old ones which may list agencies that are no longer in business. The names of agencies are sometimes a giveaway. For example, it isn't hard to work out what an agency with a name like 'Accountancy Personnel' covers. Some agencies take large display advertisements in directories in which they state quite clearly what they do. You will still be left with a lot of agencies whose activities remain a mystery to you (too many to start ringing up). At this stage leave them out.

Next, scan the job ads in your local newspaper. See which agencies seem to be advertising for people like you. Finally, take on board any personal recommendations. Do you have any friends or colleagues who have used agencies recently? Find out how they got on.

Don't register with too many agencies. It can give you two problems.

- You may be asked to attend too many interviews within a short space of time – more than your availability will stand.

- Two or more agencies may be putting you forward for the same job. This invites confusion and puts some employers off (the prospect of more than one agency claiming the fee for introducing you).

Here are a few tips on registering with agencies and getting the best results out of them.

- Make sure they understand your present situation and what you are looking for – in other words, take great pains to explain your target benchmarks. This will avoid agencies wasting your time by rooting out the wrong kind of jobs and, in turn, agencies getting fed up with you because they view you as impossible to please.

- Make sure they know how to contact you (your availability). Normally, agencies will ask you for this kind of information, but just so you appreciate the importance of this advice be aware that in many agencies you will be dealing with a Recruitment Consultant who is paid on a commission basis. Recruitment Consultants live in a fast-moving world where they need to get results for their clients (employers) and for themselves. Naturally, people who are difficult to get hold of don't appeal to Recruitment Consultants.

- Keep up contact with agencies. Give them a ring from time to time to see how they are getting on. Apart from reminding them you are still there, you might pick up a bit of feedback. Most importantly, you might pick up whether your targeting benchmarks are out of line with the market.

- Cultivate contacts in agencies. This is hard with bigger agencies where the turnover in staff can be such that you are rarely dealing with the same person twice. With small agencies, however, your contact may well be the proprietor or a partner. When you ring, ask for this person by name.

- Don't be impatient with agencies. They can access the market for you but they can't change it. If the kind of job you are looking for is thin on the ground for any reason then there is nothing an agency can do to alter the fact.

- Advise agencies if your circumstances change – if you change jobs;

if you get some additional qualifications; or if anything else happens to you which makes the original information you gave obsolete. The same applies if you change your CV and the agency has a copy of the old one. Untold problems can arise from agencies holding out-of-date information on candidates. Most important is to tell agencies if you move to a different address or change your phone number – (e.g. if you go onto cable). Forgetting to do this plays havoc with your availability.

- Disengage from agencies who ignore what you have said to them and pester you with the wrong kind of jobs. You do this by simply telling them to take you off their register. Pick out another agency and register with them instead.

- If you find you can't attend an interview with an employer which has been arranged via an agency, tell them as soon as possible. This will enable the agency to cancel the interview and arrange another time for you to go along (if this is what you want). Not turning up for interviews is unforgivable – certainly agencies won't forgive you for it. Needless to say, they won't be giving you the opportunity to let any more of their customers down.

Advertisements

Ads in newspapers and periodicals are still one of the best sources of information about jobs. The drawback, however, is that they are too accessible, which means that too many people apply for the jobs advertised. Here is a quick summary of newspapers and periodicals and their relative merits as sources.

Local newspapers

Most cities and large towns have a local evening paper. Some have a morning paper as well. The distribution areas of local papers frequently (and very conveniently) coincide with the kind of daily commuting distances which most people would consider reasonable if they had a car. So far so good. From a geographical point of view at least (local papers are well targeted), this point is greatly in their favour.

In most papers job ads divide down into display ads and small ads. Display ads are the big ones with borders round them and bits of artwork (e.g. company logos). Small ads are the ones you find in the 'Situations Vacant' columns. Small ads are usually divided down into occupational categories such as 'Managerial', 'Office Work' or 'Part-time Vacancies'. Display ads tend to be jumbled up together and can sometimes stray onto odd pages of the newspaper.

Note that most local papers have special 'jobs days' when the amount of recruitment advertising they carry increases substantially. Wednesdays and Thursdays are favourites.

If you happen to be looking for a job in a different part of the country, it is important to get your hands on the local paper that covers your targeted area. You will find the Subscriptions Departments of newspapers extremely helpful. They will be able to advise you if the newspaper has a best day for jobs and arrange for you to have a copy on subscription. It is usually best to pay by the quarter so you have the choice of cancelling or renewing the subscription every so often. Newspapers bought on subscription usually arrive the day after publication, so nothing is lost.

Free sheets

These are the sort of papers that get pushed through the door free-of-charge. Free sheets have mushroomed in the last 20 years. Advertising in free sheets is cheap (compared to evening papers) but they tend to be distributed within very small areas. Free sheets carry a fair bit of recruitment advertising, although most of it tends to be in the manual or clerical categories. As sources of career jobs free sheets perform better where there is no competition from local daily papers.

National newspapers

These divide down into the Sunday papers and the morning dailies. 'Quality' national newspapers (as opposed to tabloids) carry a lot of recruitment advertising for which they compete ferociously. Advertisements placed in national newspapers will tend to be for top managerial and professional jobs. Advertising in nationals is very expensive – each spread costs several thousand pounds.

Some national newspapers have a reputation for particular types of job. For example the *Daily Telegraph* is the traditional vehicle for top sales jobs. The *Financial Times* has much the same sort of reputation in the world of finance. Organisations keen to make an ethical or political statement may, on the other hand, prefer the *Guardian*. Competition for jobs advertised in national newspapers is bound to be intense. Another drawback is that the jobs in national newspapers can be located anywhere (not well targeted).

Professional journals

Most of the professions have their own journals which carry a fair amount of recruitment advertising. While being well targeted occupationally, these journals are national, sometimes international, publications and hence the jobs advertised in them will be located 'anywhere and everywhere'.

Trade journals

Journals which circulate within certain trades or industries can be fruitful sources of jobs. Usually these are national publications and the 'anywhere and everywhere' problem arises again.

Mix and match your reading of periodicals and newspapers, and don't be afraid to experiment. The local evening paper is a must, especially on jobs night. If you are in the 'top jobs' bracket you will be perplexed by the choice of national newspapers (Sunday and daily). You won't have time to read them all, so don't try to. Concentrate on a mix-and-match of the *Daily Telegraph*, *Financial Times*, *Observer*, *Sunday Telegraph* and *Sunday Times*, and glance at some of the others when you can.

As a general warning regarding jobs you see advertised in newspapers, don't make assumptions such as:

- 'the bigger the ad, the better the job': this certainly doesn't hold true, as good jobs are often advertised in the 'Situations Vacant' columns;
- 'firms who advertise a lot must be doing well': firms who advertise a lot include firms that can't keep their staff;

- 'an upbeat ad means an upbeat firm': most big ads are prepared by copywriters who work for advertising agencies;
- 'big ads are not worth replying to': said, presumably, because there will be too many applicants; while the observation is true, competition shouldn't stop you applying.

Advertising yourself

You will have noticed in many newspapers and periodicals a section in the small ads headed 'Employment Wanted' or something similar. People can advertise themselves in these columns. For example: 'STATISTICIAN Graduate. Female. Mid-thirties. Seeking position in East Midlands. Market research preferred. Anything around £18–£20k considered. Replies to Box No. xxx.' Tales from people who have advertised themselves in this way indicate widely varying experiences.

If you want to give advertising yourself a try, here are a few pointers that might help.

- Choose your media carefully. People who advertise themselves in professional or trade journals appear to be those who have enjoyed most success.
- Give some thought to your copy. Apart from keeping it succinct (for cost reasons) you need to get in the punch points. The example we have given is good in this respect. It tells us in one-word sentences what this person does, how old she is and what she is looking for.
- If you decide to run your ad in a local evening paper, choose jobs night. A lot of employers read the ads on jobs night.
- Don't put your phone number in your ad. Apart from cranks, there is a whole army of people out there just itching to sell you job-getting products (CVs prepared; counselling; vocational guidance; interviewing techniques, etc.). Use the newspaper's box-number facility for your replies.
- Don't be disappointed if advertising yourself doesn't work. View it as a long shot. Don't repeat the exercise.

Other sources

Sourcing methods are constantly changing: e-mail shots are already starting to creep in.

Choosing sourcing methods

Just as the market for jobs divides down into a visible (advertised) market and an invisible (unadvertised) market, so sourcing methods split between 'proactive' and 'reactive'.

Proactive sourcing methods are those where you provide the stimulus. Cold calling, mail/faxshots, networking and advertising yourself are all proactive methods. Proactive methods are the best way of accessing the unadvertised or invisible market.

Reactive methods are those where the stimulus is provided by the recruiters. Responding to advertisements is a reactive method. So is reading the boards at the local Job Centre. By definition, reactive methods focus the visible market.

Quantifying the invisible market is well nigh impossible. Viewed from a candidate's point of view, however, there are just three things to say about it:

- it exists;
- it is sizeable;
- you need to get in on it.

This is why in selecting sourcing methods you must always seek to combine proactive and reactive.

3.2 Applying for the right jobs

After sourcing jobs, you next have to decide which ones to apply for. You won't be applying for all the jobs you source. In this section we are going to look at how to decide which jobs to go for and which to leave alone. The second is as important as the first. Applying for the wrong jobs is the source of much woe.

- Attending interviews for the wrong jobs eats into your precious time-off-work time. Interviews for the right jobs come up and you

find yourself having to give them a miss because you have run out of excuses or floating holidays.
- Employers are usually quick to spot square pegs, hence the wrong jobs will be the ones you won't get. This means you are inviting discouragement.
- Interview experience will be misleading. Going for the wrong jobs could, for example, lead you into thinking quite incorrectly that the kind of job you are looking for doesn't exist. This tends to happen a lot on the question of pay. People going for a procession of poorly paid jobs will form the view that this poor level is the market rate.
- Worst of all, you may *get* the wrong job – because of omissions on your part or because the employer's selection is poor. The result could be dire (for you).

The right jobs to apply for are of course the ones which make matches with your target benchmarks – or are near enough. The wrong ones are those that don't. This sounds simple enough, and it is; but you need to apply this kind of selectivity and keep on applying it.

Blind interviews

Targeting can get problematic where you are asked along for an interview knowing nothing, or next to nothing, about the job. Blind interviews, as we call them, normally arise from particular types of sourcing activity: cold calling, mail/faxshots, networking and self-advertising – in short, proactive sourcing methods where you are providing the stimulus. They can also arise from approach situations, e.g. 'Come along and see us – we've got something interesting we want to talk to you about', where you haven't got a clue before the interview as to what the 'something interesting' might be.

Of course it would be foolish to say no to an invitation to attend a blind interview, or to say 'Hang on a minute while I go through my targeting benchmarks with you'. What you need, though, is some way of cancelling out the time-wasters.

Ian is a Health and Safety Advisor and he works for an employers' association. His problem is promotion. He is a one-man team, a specialist, and he knows if he stays where he is he stands little chance of making the next step up the ladder (to Assistant Director level). Ian is now 38.

In addition to keeping his eye on newspapers and professional journals, Ian tries doing some mailshots. He puts together a list of about 50 companies in hazardous or environmentally sensitive industries, and sends an enquiring letter and a copy of his CV to the Chief Executive of each of them. In his letter, he states that he is earning £28,000, and has the use of an association car. He says he is looking to improve on this figure and that he is happy about any location except the south of England.

Quite a few of the companies acknowledge Ian's letter but the story is usually the same – 'Thank you for your interest, but we have no suitable vacancies for you at the moment.' There is one interesting reply, however, from a firm in the mining and quarrying industry based in North Yorkshire. The letter comes from the Managing Director, a Mr Greenslade, and it gives him a time and date to come along for a preliminary interview.

Intrigued, Ian books the day off and makes the journey up to North Yorkshire. At the interview Mr Greenslade is cordial enough. He explains to Ian that the firm has grown quite rapidly over the last 15 years, mainly by acquisition. It now has over 40 mining and quarrying sites in the UK alone. The need that has arisen – and it was fortuitous Ian's CV landed on Mr Greenslade's desk when it did – is for a Head Office-based Health and Safety Co-ordinator who will provide advice and support to the UK Regional Management team. Ian asks if the job has been advertised. Mr Greenslade says it hasn't. Salary is discussed. Mr Greenslade says the Group has a figure of around £30,000 in mind, and a car will be provided, since extensive travel is envisaged. There will be a relocation package, too.

Ian nods along, but the more Mr Greenslade talks the more Ian realises this isn't what he wants. It isn't a step up the ladder but another one-man-band job rather like the one he's got. True, the pay is a bit better, but not much; and for this he will be taking on more risk. He will be moving into the unknown, moving to a strange part of the country, and moving into a commercial environment where there is bound to be less security. As soon as it is polite to say so, Ian explains all of this. Mr Greenslade seems slightly taken aback. Ian apologises. They shake hands, and Ian leaves.

On his way back home, Ian ponders the day's events. It has all been a waste of time really – a waste of Mr Greenslade's time and a waste of his own. Ian wonders if it is his fault.

Ian shouldn't be too self-reproachful. We all learn from experience, and his mistake was one plenty of people make. In his mailshot he did not make it clear what he was looking for. He set out his salary expectations and defined areas of the country he would not be happy to move to, but he did not explain the most important fact about why he was putting himself on the market – namely that he was looking for a bigger job, something at least equivalent to an Assistant Director's job in the employers' association. Of course, there was no way poor Mr Greenslade could know this, so Ian was really to blame for ending up in an interview for a job which fell way short of his targeting.

In any proactive sourcing you do – in particular cold calling and mail/faxshots – you must keep up the proactivity and spell out precisely what you are trying to achieve. You cannot, of course, legislate for employers who don't listen or don't take in what they read, but nine times out of ten you will find that setting out your stall properly will avert the sort of situation Ian found himself in. In fact, next time you get asked along to a blind interview you will be able to feel reasonably sure (as sure as you can be) that the job the employer wants to talk to you about is something that is going to be interesting.

Approach is a slightly different kettle of fish. By definition, approach is unsolicited, unasked for, and you will have had no opportunity up to the point of contact to explain your situation to anyone. Furthermore, an approacher may not want to talk over the phone. He/she may suggest a preliminary meeting, the purpose of which will be to sound you out. Here again the preliminary meeting could prove to be a complete waste of time. For example, the approacher may be looking at a job which pays only half your salary.

How do you avoid it? The answer is that you can't, and here we would urge you to take the risk. Go along and see what you learn. There are three reasons for this advice.

- You won't be approached very often. In other words, having your time wasted by approachers won't be a recurring event.
- Some good jobs come from approach.
- There is usually scope for negotiation, particularly on points of salary and perks.

Advertisements without salaries

Ads without salaries are a major obstacle in the way of candidates' targeting. If you don't know the pay, how do you know whether a job's worth applying for or not? Let's start by examining why companies don't put salaries in ads.

- They may not want all and sundry knowing what salaries they pay.
- They may be fishing in the dark. They may not have the faintest idea what salary to pin on the job being advertised, simply because of ignorance of market rates. They may want to see what you're earning first, so they know whether they can afford you or not. (This approach is typical of smaller firms.)
- They pay poor salaries and they don't like to say.

The way to get round ads without salaries is by making your pay expectation clear in your CV and letter of application (we will be looking at letters of application shortly). An employer who sees that you are after £2,000 a year more than they can afford won't invite you to an interview. It is as simple as that.

The snag is, of course, that you won't get any feedback from the experience. You won't learn anything from the letter you get turning you down, and there is a problem for you here.

'Sorry' and 'No thank you' letters (not being invited to the interview) are a separate subject which we will be dealing with later on (see page 113). Suffice it to say at this stage that 'Sorry' and 'No thank you' letters should not be regarded without exception as evidence of failure. Candidates who are too good for the job will get 'Sorry' and 'No thank you' letters in just the same way as candidates who are completely unsuitable. So, if you are not asked along for an interview, take it that 50 per cent of the time it will be the job and not you that is falling short of the mark. There are plenty of things in employment to get depressed about – 'Sorry' and 'No thank you' letters aren't one of them. Targeting jobs and doing it properly will in any event reduce the number of 'Sorry' and 'No thank you' letters you will be getting.

There is an important side issue here that we need to deal with. There are some clear dangers for the unemployed in stating pay expectations that are too high. At the onset of unemployment, people tend to set their sights on getting back into the sort of job they have just left, and set their targeting benchmarks accordingly – including pay. Of course, the average person has no way of knowing whether his or her last job was well paid or badly paid or somewhere in the middle. But, as unemployment drags on, the question arises: 'Am I asking for too much?' Let's take a look at a case study.

> Betty is 42. She got made redundant from the local council last year. At the time, she felt reasonably confident about getting another job. She was used to working with computerised information systems and she had five years' supervisory experience. Her pay with the council was £15,000. Betty set her sights on getting an Office Supervisor's job in an insurance company or a firm of chartered accountants, or similar. She figured that salaries outside local government might be lower so she put a figure of £14,000 on her pay expectation. Betty is a widow with a mortgage to pay and two children still in full-time education.
>
> Betty prepared her own CV. She made a point of keeping her eyes on the jobs in the local paper and, in addition to regular visits to the Job Centre, she registered with three agencies. Four months ago she tried a mailshot. She targeted professional offices, asking if they had any vacancies for supervisors paying £14,000 or more. All

this activity yielded absolutely nothing – not even an interview.

Betty drew the conclusion that she was asking for too much money. With the redundancy cash she got from the council dwindling rapidly, she decided to re-do her CV, leaving out any mention of pay expectations. She visited the agencies again and told them to cut the frills and find her 'anything reasonable'.

Two weeks ago, Betty saw a job advertised in a licensed Betting Office and she applied. She had an interview with the manager who offered her the job starting at £3.85 an hour rising to £4.20 after a month's trial. Now she is in a quandary. £4.20 an hour is a far cry from £14,000 a year but, with overtime, she knows she will be better off than she is on benefits, so can she really afford to turn the offer down? What's bothering Betty, though, is that the job won't solve the financial problems. There will still be a shortfall between her incomings and her outgoings. She really needs to be earning £12,000 a year to stay buoyant.

Is £14,000 too much to be asking? Possibly not. It all depends on Betty's local job market. The obvious problems with Betty's targeting are that:

- there probably isn't much demand for supervisors in professional offices (the target is too narrow);
- there will be a marked preference for people with experience of whatever the commercial activity happens to be (a large insurance office with a vacancy for a supervisor will, for example, want someone who knows something about insurance – not an ex-local government official).

Yet we cannot be critical of Betty for not being able to see the problems for herself. Most of us learn about our own particular niche of the job market from our experiences. Betty's trouble is that, because her targeting is narrow, she is getting no experience. She is learning nothing. She hasn't attended any interviews for supervisory jobs, hence she has no feedback. Because she is out of work and her whole way of life is under threat, she is naturally starting to panic. She tries to deduce for herself where she is going wrong.

She seizes on pay rather than the narrowness of her target. Really she is doing no more than stabbing in the dark, but what else can she do? She has no experience from which she can draw a more accurate conclusion.

The point of this case study is to illustrate what unemployed people tend to do in these situations: drop their targeting benchmarks altogether and go for anything and everything. In other words, their whole approach falls apart. What poor Betty clearly hasn't tested is the market for non-supervisory office jobs paying around £12,000. Again, these may or may not be available – but Betty will never find out because time has run out on her.

If you are out of work, the rules for flagging up your pay expectations to prospective employers are different to those for people in jobs. You must still do it, and this is important. If you don't, you will find most of the interviews you attend will be for what you will view as poorly paid jobs. The effect of this is discouraging and demoralising, i.e. not what unemployed people need. There is a further problem for you, too: you will begin to form the opinion – incorrectly – that these poor levels of pay are the market rate. You will then be drawn towards taking such jobs (just like Betty) because you feel there is no alternative.

We all need to be flexible about our pay expectations, and the unemployed need to be more flexible than anyone else. Their learning curve has to be much shorter too. People in jobs can afford to take months and years getting their targeting benchmarks right. The unemployed don't have this luxury. Not only will financial pressures start to bear down on them but the stigma of long-term unemployment quickly begins to creep in. Employers take a jaundiced view of people who have been out of work a long time, and there is no escaping this. The great window of opportunity for the out-of-work is in the first few months of unemployment. After this the window starts to close. Getting a good job becomes more and more difficult. Anyone who has been out of work for long periods will confirm this. If, like Betty, you are staking everything in the first few months on a single narrow target, then you may well be courting disaster for yourself.

Betty's case is interesting because it illustrates the benefits that can be derived from multiple targeting during the 'window of opportunity' (the period preceding unemployment and the first few months when you are out of work). In particular, it illustrates what can be gained from a 'high bid/low bid' approach. In Betty's case, the high bid is an Office Supervisor's job paying £14,000. The low bid is a £12,000 clerical job with information-technology skills. The key is to go for both. So, in effect, Betty can be pursuing two quite separate sourcing exercises. 'Multiple targeting' means that two isn't the limit, either – you can go for any number of targets (depending on your range of experience/skills). In fact, the more targets the merrier. This is where candidates may require more than one CV.

Maximum effort (application) must be put into the 'window of opportunity' period. Success, of course, can't be guaranteed, but after three or four months of this kind of busy yet targeted activity you will at least have experience on which to base future decisions – and you may even land yourself a good job along the way.

Here are a few don'ts for people facing unemployment.

- Don't delay in getting yourself on the market. Don't wait until you are finished (which is what a lot of people do).

- Don't think you are going to get another (comparable) job straight away. It will make you complacent, and complacency is dangerous. If anything, expect the worst.

- Don't think a big redundancy pay-off buys you time. People with several thousand pounds in their pockets can be lulled into thinking they don't have to do anything for a few months. Take it from us – the stigma of being unemployed gets bigger as time passes. Remember the window of opportunity and how soon it closes. With unemployment, time is never on your side.

- Don't be side-tracked. A favourite option is to spend the first few months of unemployment investigating the feasibility of going on college courses. By the time people discover they don't have the resources, the window of opportunity has passed them by.

- Don't take a holiday. Going off for a month in the south of France with the caravan ('I'll never get another chance like this') fouls up your all-important accessibility/availability. Get some sense of urgency into you. Panic now and you may not be panicking in six months' time when your window of opportunity has closed.

- Don't pursue single targets like Betty did, because they might be too narrow (you have no way of knowing). Pursue as many targets as possible (consistent with your skills and experience). Consider all options. Use your ability to take risks as fully as possible.
- Don't go for anything and everything (i.e. fail to target). This is the road to discouragement. You can do without discouragement.

LESSON 3 Keeping control

You will have gathered by now that we are using these little lessons to introduce you to the fundamental principles of career power in the kind of difficult market conditions we have to live with today. We have looked at the three As — accessibility, availability and application. We have also looked at first impressions. In this lesson we will be looking at control and how to keep it.

We hear a lot about control freaks. Control in careers is about keeping you in control of events, as much as possible.

Selection, done properly, is a painful and time-consuming business. Not surprisingly, it doesn't appeal to today's manager in a hurry who has to operate with limited resources. The inclination will be to shortcut the process. The bottom line in this set of circumstances is that selecting someone for a job has to be fitted in between a lot of other conflicting pressures. As a result, it is rarely done properly.

In our first lesson we examined how selection carried out in modern conditions can work to the advantage of candidates who offer accessibility, availability and application. The same goes for candidates who take control.

It used to be employers who said: 'Don't ring us, we'll ring you.' In modern employment conditions we need to get this the other way round. As a general rule in selection, things that are left at a loose end are things that tend to fall down the slot. Managers who are up to their ears in day-to-day problems forget to do things, or put them off. If they promise to phone a candidate, or write to them by a certain date, there is a chance they won't. The candidate will be left waiting and wondering.

The suggestion is of course to turn the tables. If you are the candidate, then you should be the one ringing up and making the running. This is just one example of keeping control. We will be seeing a number of others as we go along.

3.3 Replying to advertisements

You will source some jobs from newspaper ads. Once you have satisfied yourself that a job matches your targeting benchmarks, you will want to apply. Replying to newspaper ads is the next subject we will look at.

Facing up to competition

Replying to ads means attacking the visible market, where competition is going to be toughest and where somehow you have got to make yourself stand out from the crowd. Your aim, remember, is to get an interview. Now imagine some hard-pressed manager who has just run an ad in the local press and has dozens and dozens of applications to read through. How do you get yourself noticed by this person?

Your accessibility is obviously the key here. This, you will remember, is the clarity with which you come across: the extent to which you pass or fail the one-read test. Anything you put in front of an employer – letters, CV, application forms – must therefore be capable of standing up to this kind of treatment. What you have got to offer has got to be understood first time, because it won't get another chance.

The other half of the equation is that what you have to offer has to match up to what the employer is looking for. What comes across to our hard-pressed employer must be something he or she actually wants.

So how do you find out what an employer is looking for? Well, for a start, ads usually contain clues: 'The ideal candidate will have . . . ', 'This position calls for someone with . . . ', and so on. There is often a description of the job itself – the duties and responsibilities – and in these descriptions there will be further indications as to the sort of candidate considered suitable.

Reading through ads carefully (which few candidates do) will help you pick out the strong points in your application. Strong points could include:

- that you are in the right age group;
- that you hold the right qualifications;
- that you have the right kind of experience;
- that you have received a particular kind of training;
- that you have the kind of personal qualities the employer is seeking;
- that you live in the right place.

Whatever they are, your strong points are what need to be brought out and given prominence. It doesn't matter if you don't have all the attributes listed in the ad, but the ones you do have need to be brought to the fore. At the application stage there are three potential vehicles for conveying your strong points:

- your letter of application;
- your CV;
- any application forms you fill in.

We will be looking at each of these in turn later, but in passing please note that bringing your strong points into prominence is yet another way of keeping control. In this case, you are controlling what the employer picks up in a quick read of your application. You are controlling the fact that this is information that will figure in your favour.

Following instructions

There is a clear code of practice to follow when replying to ads: do exactly what the ad asks you to do and not something else. Typical ways in which candidates fall down are:

- sending in a CV when the ad asks you to ring in for an application form;
- ringing in when the ad asks for applications in writing;
- ignoring closing dates;
- not quoting reference codes (consultants and large companies tend to use reference codes in their ads as a way of quickly identifying which ad a candidate is replying to. The consultant or company may be running several different ads for several different jobs and in several different newspapers);
- sending a letter saying 'I enclose my CV . . . ' and failing to do so (commoner than you think).

At best, transgressions such as these will lead to delays in processing your application. At worst, they will mean your application finishing up in the bin.

Most ads these days simply ask you to send in a CV. Alternatively, they ask you to apply in writing giving details of age, qualifications and experience to date, etc., which you can safely interpret as meaning send in your CV. If you've followed the advice so far, you will have a stock of CVs ready prepared. The importance of this is now revealed. There must be no delay in getting your application off. Not having a CV to hand is a common cause of delay.

Ads may not state a closing date (most of them don't), but as a rule of thumb take it that applications received more than five working days after the advertisement has appeared will stand a reduced chance of being read.

Delay in getting off applications is often caused simply by procrastination (lack of application) – 'I'll do it tomorrow' – and this is unforgivable. Three don'ts are worth mentioning here.

- Don't use second-class mail.
- Don't forget that letters weighing more than 60g require extra postage.
- Don't outsmart yourself by delivering your application by hand.

Candidates wouldn't do this if they knew how many applications turned up months later in the bottom drawers of receptionists' desks.

Letters of application

Sending in your CV will require an accompanying letter. Letters of application provide you with an opportunity to bring your strong points into prominence. Other things to bear in mind when it comes to writing letters of application are as follows.

- Make it clear which job you are applying for by reference to the job title (the one used in the ad) and to the newspaper in which it appeared. If a reference code is given, then quote it.

- Briefly describe your current situation and what you are looking for – particularly regarding pay (especially if the ad doesn't quote a salary).

- Set out your availability – best times to phone you; availability for interviews (even though this is repeated in your CV).

- Make sure your letter is accessible – easy to understand.

- Check your spelling!

An example of a letter of application is shown opposite.

There are two interesting points to note in this letter.

- The second paragraph, where John sets out his strong points. Nifty Nimble's ad stated a preference for graduates mid-20s to early 30s with 'several years in systems' and with experience of the software John refers to. The job involves travel so the mobility was stressed, as well as the need to be able to prioritise (Nifty Nimble's systems department is obviously very busy). 'Mobile' and 'Prioritise' were the actual words Nifty Nimble used in the ad. Words are important in application letters. Companies hear echoes of their own thinking if you use their words. It gets your strong points across immediately. Your own choice of words for the same thing won't have such impact. What is more, in this world of ever-increasing buzzwords and jargon, there is a chance that companies won't be

18 March 1997

18 Acacia Gardens
Anytown AT99 9XX

Mr B Fisher
Financial Director
Nifty Nimble Dietary Products Limited
Othertown OT99 9ZZ

Dear Mr Fisher

   Systems Co-ordinator (Ref BBF/111/EB)

I wish to apply for the position advertised in tonight's Evening Bugle. A copy of my CV is enclosed.

Please note that:
- I am a 28-year-old graduate with five years' experience in systems development and installation.
- I am fully conversant with Microsoft software.
- I am fully mobile and hold a clean driving licence.
- I am used to facing conflicting demands and to having to prioritise my work and the work of my staff.

My present company is undergoing major restructuring and my position is due to become redundant at the end of the year. I am earning £17,250 p.a. and ideally I would be looking for around the same.

You can contact me in the office on 01123 456789 (extension 45) or at home on 01123 987654 (after 6.30pm). I can attend for interview at any time given a few days' notice and I have been told that I can be released immediately (i.e. before my redundancy date) if I am successful in finding another job.

Yours sincerely

John Southall

enc: CV

familiar with your word in the context you use it, i.e. you run the risk of not being understood (accessibility fails).

- Because of his circumstances, John is remarkably available. He has made good use of the letter to advertise this fact.

It is acceptable for an application letter to be handwritten, providing of course it is neat. If your letter is typed, make sure you sign it. Use black ink on white plain A4 paper (as with your CV). Apart from anything else, this ensures your letter will fax and photocopy well. A fountain pen or a thin fibre-tip always looks better than a ballpoint. Either keep a copy of your application letter, or make a careful note of what you have said. (Find out why when we come on to keeping records on page 105.)

Customising your CV

This is where the home-PC buffs come into their own. You can get your CV up on screen and change it to match the job you are applying for. In particular, you can bring your strong points to the fore (your little personal profile is a good place for getting these in). Print off an extra copy of your customised CV for your records.

Faxing in your application

Companies sometimes advertise the facility to fax in applications. Sometimes candidates take it upon themselves to use fax instead of post – the motive being that it looks slicker and it gets their application in first.

As a general rule, we would say that, if you have a choice, don't fax in applications for the following reasons.

- Faxes don't look particularly good. They roll up and they crinkle, and they don't take good photocopies. As a result, first impressions suffer.

- With faxes there is always the risk a page will be lost or a several-page document will be assembled in the wrong order when it reaches the other end. In short, you surrender control.

Some ads may instruct you to fax in your CV. If this is what they want, then do as you are told. This is where having your CV typed in black, on white A4 paper, will help. It will fax well.

Application forms

Not all employers use application forms, but a good percentage of them do. Certainly most bigger firms have a standard application form. Use black ink to fill in application forms (blue ink doesn't photocopy well and your application form may have to survive being photocopied several times during the selection process). Except for the simple bits, draft what you are going to say before you actually commit pen to paper, and check your spelling at the same time! If you do make a mistake, cross it out with a single straight line using a ruler. Don't try rubbing out or blobbing with correcting fluid.

A few other points to bear in mind when completing application forms are as follows.

- Fill in all the sections/answer all the questions and don't leave blanks. If, for example, there is a question asking you for details of any endorsements on your driving licence, and you don't have any, then write in 'None'.

- Sign the form – if this is required. Some people have got a 'thing' about putting their signatures to forms. In the case of application forms, not signing could be taken as an indication of awkwardness or meaning the information on the form isn't true.

- Make sure that the answers you give on the form are consistent with information contained in your CV, because discrepancies tend to be noticed. Dates when periods of employment began and ended are the most common form of discrepancy.

- Keep your responses as short as possible. Space alone often means you will have no alternative. But if there is a big space for a reply to a question don't feel you have to fill it. Rather like your CV, an application form has to stand the one-read (accessibility) test.

- The application form is another opportunity to plug your strong points. Refer back to the ad and make sure, for example, you include anything you have done in any of your jobs which is consistent with what the employer is looking for. Remember, again, to use words the employer uses. Some application forms have a section headed 'Any further information relevant to your application', or words to that effect. This is the ideal place to list your strong points.

- Enclose a copy of your CV with the application form. The two read together will give a better picture of you. This applies even if you have previously submitted a CV. Here is yet another example of keeping control – you are taking responsibility for ensuring your application form and CV are paired together. You haven't left it up to someone at the other end to find time to forage for your CV in last week's mail.
- Include a covering letter with your application form and CV.
- Buy some clear A4 plastic folders. A plastic folder will serve to keep your CV, application form and letter together (more control).
- Take a photocopy of the completed application form. Memory fades fast and it may be several weeks before you are invited to an interview. An interviewer will have your completed form on the desk and will be referring to it. Hence, as part of your preparations for interviews, you need to read through any application forms you have submitted because your answers to questions need to be consistent with what you have put on the form.
- Don't delay in sending your application form off. Use first-class post, and checking the weight is essential this time. The application form, your CV and letter, plus the weight of a plastic folder, is probably going to come to more than 60g, i.e. additional postage will be required.

3.4 Applications for jobs sourced proactively

Proactive sourcing, you will recall, is where you do the initiating. Proactive sourcing methods include cold calling, mail/faxshots, networking and advertising yourself. Proactive sourcing enables you to access the invisible market where competition will be considerably less and sometimes non-existent.

The halo effect

Remember what we had to say about early impressions? Professional interviewers are trained to be wary of the so-called halo effect: the tendency to see some good points in a candidate early on in the selection process and from there on to ignore any flaws which may arise. Halo effects are most common where:

- there is only one candidate for a job and hence it will benefit the employer greatly if this candidate just happens to be right;
- there is pressure on the employer to find someone quickly.

Because of the halo effect, suitable candidates who have sourced jobs proactively stand an extremely good chance of being successful.

Thinking on your feet

One aspect of proactive sourcing which candidates can find disturbing is the speed at which things happen. You can find yourself whisked into an interview, at the end of which you can find the interviewer offering you the job.

There is a fine line between being rushed into decisions and looking gift horses in the mouth. Part and parcel of being a proactive sourcer is having the ability to know instantly when you've been offered a good job – knowing when to say 'Yes', when to say 'No', and when to say 'I'd like to think it over'. There are two keys to this.

- Think through your targeting benchmarks properly, and do this beforehand so that you have some ready yardsticks by which to judge jobs.
- Listen to what your instincts tell you about the job and the person offering it to you (more on trusting your instincts later).

3.5 Keeping records of your applications

This is very necessary, for the simple reason that several weeks can elapse between making applications and going to interviews.

Interviewers flick through candidates' papers before they see them, and it pays candidates to do the same. There are some famous interview howlers – candidates with puzzled looks on their faces saying 'Which version of my CV have you got?' or 'Where did I say that?' Avoid situations like these by keeping copies of any documents you submit, notably:

- any letters of application;
- your CV (remember, if you alter your CV, to keep copies of the old one);
- any application forms you have filled in.

If the job was advertised, cut the ad out of the paper and staple it onto your copy documents. Make a note of when you sent an application off (the date you posted it), and of any subsequent events (phone calls, interviews, etc.). In short, build up a little dossier on each application.

Summary

These days only a proportion of good jobs are ever advertised or become visible in other ways. The principal reason is that small to medium-sized firms, which make up so much of today's market, don't have dedicated Personnel or Human Resources specialists to organise recruitment for them. Recruitment will be handled by a multitude of individual managers who have other demands on their time and only limited expertise. For these reasons they view running advertisements, sifting through piles of applications and interviewing and re-interviewing a number of candidates with a mixture of apprehension and dread. Inevitably, they look for short-cuts or 'other ways'.

Even in large firms Personnel Departments are frequently just shadows of their former selves. Seen in recessionary times as non-essential overheads, they have often been cut down or even completely axed. The tendency throughout is for more and more responsibility for recruiting to be pressed onto under-resourced line managers.

There has always been an unadvertised or invisible market but it has flourished and grown in the kind of conditions we have just described. Furthermore, as we all know, the pace of business life has quickened with the need to be more competitive and with the availability of ever-improving information technology. In consequence, there is today an urgency about recruiting, a need to get vacancies filled fast, and this too has had an eroding effect on the visible market.

Drafting an advertisement, waiting for 'jobs night' to come round in the local evening paper, waiting for the replies to come in and so on is too long-winded for firms in a hurry. So what do they do when a need to fill a vacancy arises?

- Approach offers one quick solution and saves the rigmarole of advertising and having to interview a lot of candidates.

- Employment agencies offer another quick route. They can carry out a search of their files and put forward a selection of suitable candidates within a relatively short period of time. It has a cost, but again the rigmarole of having to go through a lot of candidates is avoided.

- Then there is what employers regard as the stroke of luck – the suitable candidate who, by chance, just happens to phone or send in a CV.

Sourcing good jobs means you have to tackle both markets – the visible and the invisible. Too many candidates concentrate their efforts on newspaper advertisements and give little or no attention to the invisible market. Its seeming inaccessibility puts them off. In consequence, they undersource.

Of course you won't be applying for all the jobs you source. You will need to run a little test over them first. Without being pedantic you will need to establish, insofar as you can, that the jobs you are going to apply for match up to your targeting benchmarks. This selectivity is all-important.

How you go about applying for jobs depends on how you sourced them.

Proactively sourced jobs

Proactive sourcing is aimed at the invisible market. The idea is that, by being methodical with proactive sourcing, you present yourself to an employer at precisely the right time – the right time being when the employer has a need.

With proactively sourced jobs, there are two things you need to watch.

- Make sure the employer is reading you correctly. Your CV and anything you say or write about yourself must communicate your aims and expectations (including pay) clearly and unambiguously (accessibility). This is your defence against employers assuming that you want to apply for jobs that are completely wrong. (Ian the Health and Safety Expert fell into this category.)

- Be careful not to be swept off your feet by the sheer pace of events. Know what you want before you start. Know when to say yes.

Reactively sourced jobs

These are jobs you see advertised. Here the problem is competition, and in making applications you need to take account of this. You are attacking the visible market and any good job which surfaces onto the visible market will attract large numbers of applications.

In such circumstances being 'suitable' won't necessarily guarantee you an interview. Three other factors come into play, two of which we have covered in Chapter 2: your accessibility and your availability. The employer must be able to see in one glance that you are suitable, which brings into play the accessibility of your CV, any forms you fill in and any letters of application you send off. The employer has also got to be able to get hold of you – you have got to be contactable by phone without fuss and you have got to be able to go to the interviews (your availability).

The third factor is really an enhancement of your accessibility: bringing out your strong points for the job – making yourself stand out from the rest. Vehicles for strong points are again your CV (suitably customised), any letters you write and any forms you fill in.

Bringing out your strong points is also an important aspect of what we have described as keeping control: in this case controlling what the employers take in from a quick read of your information and ensuring that this is favourable.

Questions and answers

Cold calling – feeling a nuisance

Q *I don't like cold calling companies. I feel I'm pestering people and being a nuisance.*

A Look at it this way: advertising jobs, using agencies or consultants all cost companies a lot of money. If you happen to be just what they are looking for, then you will be saving them a sizeable sum – and if anyone is really funny with you then give them a zero score on your scale of ratings (they're not worth the time of day). This means you won't be ringing them again.

Applying for the right jobs – not enough jobs match my target

Q *I am a secretary with language skills (notably French and Italian). I am looking for a job where I can use my languages to greater advantage and I am targeting secretarial jobs in multinationals or UK companies with big EU markets. I am currently secretary to the Chairman and Managing Director of a vehicle-leasing company where there is an occasional – very occasional – need to speak to our one French client. I scan the ads in the local evening paper every night and I am registered with one staff agency. I earn £16,000 at the moment, which is the sort of figure I want to match (I might take a slight drop in salary if the job looks really promising).*

I have been looking for the last 12 months but so far only three suitable jobs have come up. (I was shortlisted for all of them but each time someone pipped me to the post.) Three jobs doesn't strike me as being very many, and I want to know if I am doing anything wrong. For instance, should I be toning down my pay expectations, or should I be widening my net to take in other areas of commerce?

A Perhaps, but the root problem you seem to have is in your sourcing. Flicking through the evening paper and being registered with a staff agency sounds like undersourcing. In particular, you seem to be missing out on any proactive sourcing. Also top-flight secretarial jobs don't tend to get advertised that much. The bulk of them never surface onto the visible market and you will probably only ever access them via specialist agencies or by other proactive methods. Here is our suggested plan of action.

- Ask yourself: is the agency you are using really the right one? A lot of staff agencies are temp-orientated. What you need is the kind of agency that handles top secretarial appointments. Check your local business directories. Check which agencies are generally advertising good secretarial jobs. Do you know any other secretaries? See if they can suggest a good agency.
- Try a bit of cold calling or mailing.

See this action plan through before you start tampering with your targeting benchmarks. Remember, too, that the idea of targeting is that you won't be applying for dozens of jobs. View it as a virtue that only a handful come up to specification. Straying away from your targets and applying for the wrong jobs altogether will gain you nothing.

Replying to ads – not having all the qualifications required

Q *I saw a super job advertised in the paper the other evening. Everything about it was right – salary, type of work, prospects and, as a bonus, it was located quite close to home. Then I read through the qualifications and experience needed and my heart sank. There was a big long list. I had done some of the things but not all of them. Should I apply or will I be wasting my time?*

A Make sure first of all that this is a job you can do and that you are not over-reaching. Be honest with yourself. There may be good reason for the big long list of requirements. On the other hand, organisations sometimes fall into the trap of over-specifying jobs and finding that no one applies (apart from the sort of people who apply for every job they see advertised).

If you feel you can do the job and if it meets your targeting benchmarks (it sounds like it does) then our view would be to have a go. This is a case where you have got to get your strong points to the fore. You never know your luck with jobs which have been over-specified. A lot of the more suitable candidates may have been put off by the formidable list of requirements (like you nearly were).

Jobs you've applied for before

Q *Twelve months ago I applied for a job with a big company. I had a preliminary interview and got turned down. Now the same company is advertising again. Is it worth my while applying? If so, should I be reminding them of my previous application?*

A If a week is a long time in politics, 12 months is an eternity in employment. We know plenty of cases of people who have been turned down by companies then gone on to be successful second time around. Don't worry about telling them you've been interviewed before. It's unlikely they'll remember you anyway. Apply, unless they have actually stated in their ad that they don't want to hear from previous applicants.

Hearing nothing from an agency

Q *I registered with an agency two months ago. I have heard nothing from them since. I presume they have forgotten about me.*

A Give them a chance. If they are working to your targeting benchmarks (which is what you have asked them to do), two months is no time at all for you to be forming harsh judgements.

Do make contact with them (as we recommend), though, and find out what is going on. For instance, there is always the possibility that your targeting benchmarks are out of line with the market, i.e. you are asking the agency to find you a job that doesn't exist. Agencies can be culpable of not feeding this kind of information back – unless someone asks them.

The time to start worrying about agencies is when they keep ringing you up with jobs that are completely unsuitable.

FOUR

Going for Interviews

Most of what we have done up to now has been to do with getting interviews. Getting interviews is the first step on the road to getting jobs. Interviews themselves have another function. They provide a way to build up knowledge of our own particular niche of the job market. We learn from our interview experience. We learn whether:

- we are over-reaching, taking a step too far and applying for jobs we can't do;
- the kind of jobs we are applying for have got hidden snags – things we didn't expect;
- our pay expectations are realistic and in line with what the market has to offer.

We can use our interview experience to develop our targeting benchmarks and to give them the fine-tuning they need.

4.1 Not getting interviews

Candidates who don't get interviews not only don't get jobs, but they are also deprived of any interview experience. This is what happened to Betty in our case study earlier on. Candidates who don't get interviews also feel they have failed, but this isn't necessarily the case. There are many reasons why candidates don't get interviews. For instance, candidates who are regarded by employers as too good for the job don't get interviews.

Is there a time to start worrying about the number of interviews you are getting? It's hard to say (it depends a lot on the marketability of your experience and skills) but, to pick on a completely arbitrary figure, we suggest you take a look at what you are doing if your strike rate is less than 25 per cent. If it is, then work your way through the following checklist. It should help to pinpoint the problems – if there are any.

- Are your applications long shots? Read through section 2.1 again. Are you trying to get promotion into a job with responsibilities you have never had before? Are you trying to change career? This is not a hint for you to stop what you're doing, but rather a reminder that, with speculative applications, not getting an interview should be viewed as the norm – particularly on the visible market where you will be competing against candidates with experience.

- Is your CV up to scratch? In particular, is it accessible? A way to test this is to get a second opinion from someone – preferably someone who doesn't know you too well. If this someone has had experience of employing people, then so much the better. Common problems with CVs are their length (too long), their style (messy), and their lack of conciseness (too much detail). Incidentally, by getting you to revisit your CV in this way we are not inviting you to twiddle and tweak. If the points you pick out are only minor ones, then leave it alone.

- Check out your availability again. Do the kind of availability audit we suggested on page 61. Being contactable by phone is critical to getting interviews. The practice of many employers is to whizz through a pile of applications, pick out a few suitable candidates, and then ring them up. The ones they make contact with are the ones who get invited in; the ones they don't get put to one side.

- When replying to advertisements in newspapers, are you following the rules? Are you getting your applications off quickly and by first-class post? Are you getting your strong points to the fore and ensuring you stand out from the competition?

- Are you putting too much emphasis on reactive sourcing (replying to advertisements) where the competition is greatest and where the chances of getting interviews are slimmest?
- Are you chasing narrow targets (like Betty)?

If you have gone through the checklist and are still no wiser as to why you are not getting interviews, then by a process of elimination you have arrived at the point where you need to ask yourself if your pay expectation is out of line with the market. In short, are you looking for too much money? At some point, you may have to face up to the fact that the market won't pay you what you want. Before you reach this conclusion, however:

- work your way through all the other possible explanations for not getting interviews;
- see what you can do to find out about pay levels in your part of the world. Employment agencies are not a bad source. They work at the sharp end so they should be able to tell you if you are looking for too much – providing you ask them, of course. Ads with salaries will help you too.

Ultimately, you have a choice. You can, if it is acceptable to you, tweak your pay expectations down a notch or two and see if it gets you any more interviews. The other option is to carry on with your original pay expectation but take on board that you are attacking a very narrow target (the top end of the market). The corollary to this is that you should view lack of success as the norm and not get too despondent about it. Funnily enough, the modern market has more to offer top-end targeters than the market of 15–20 years ago (which was very much tuned to 'going rates' – the rates the big firms in the district paid). The modern market is a great deal more fragmented and made up of a lot of small employers who compete quite ferociously for business and people.

4.2 Types of interview

Given that no two interviews are alike, they tend to fall into broad categories. These categories are determined by:

- how you got the interview (did you reply to an ad or did it arise from your proactive sourcing?);
- who is doing the interview.

Preliminary interviews

Good jobs which are advertised in newspapers, or which reach the visible market by other means, will attract a lot of interest. Employers faced with dozens of candidates will feel a need to whittle them down. At these whittling-down or preliminary interviews, the interviewer will be seeking to establish 'broad suitability' rather than to whom to offer the job.

Preliminary interviews will be carried out either by the firm's Personnel/Human Resources Department (if there is one), by an outside selection consultant, or by the line manager in whose area the job is based. In smaller firms it is more likely to be the last.

Most preliminary interviews are one-on-ones: the interviewer and the candidate are present and no one else. Preliminary interviews are normally kept short – 45 minutes is a fairly typical length to expect. It is also quite common for candidates to be seen in procession, one after the other. Hence, if one interview over-runs its allotted time, every other interview that day will start late.

From the interviewer's point of view, doing a procession of preliminary interviews is pretty boring stuff. It is a case of saying the same thing over and over again to candidate after candidate. Even experienced interviewers tend to flag or go into robotic mode.

Preliminary interviews for very senior jobs will be more elaborate affairs – particularly if a firm of selection consultants has been retained. Expect a psychometric test (either at the interview or on a separate occasion). Don't be surprised, either, if they want to video you. This can be unnerving, particularly if you haven't been forewarned.

Shortlist interviews

Once the preliminary interviews have taken place, some of the candidates (the shortlist) will be asked to come back for a second showing. There could be more than one shortlist interview, reflecting either indecision ('Let's take a look at them all again') or a further whittling-down (e.g. from six to two). A shortlist interview will tend to be longer than a preliminary interview. The employer will be hoping to make a selection this time, so more ground needs to be covered. A line manager (the person who would be your boss if you got the job) is normally the principal interviewer and this person clearly has to be satisfied that.

- you can do the job;
- you will fit in with the team/situation.

These are, of course, highly subjective judgements – one person's view of another.

With more senior jobs where management selection consultants have carried out the preliminary interviews, it is not unknown for them to be in attendance again at the shortlist stage. They may indeed lead the questioning or chair the selection panel, i.e. play quite an active role. If a management selection consultant has shortlisted you, you can take it for granted this person is going to be 'on your side'. Indeed consultants have been known to rescue candidates who start to flounder in final interviews. We say this to condition you to take cues from consultants who are 'sitting in'. A question will often be asked to repair an omission or some damage you have inflicted on yourself unknowingly.

Interviews arising from proactive sourcing

Sourcing jobs on the invisible market, using mail/faxshots or making cold calls (proactive sourcing), is designed to bring you into contact with employers at precisely their time of need and before they take any steps to find a replacement by advertising the job or contacting agencies. Interviews arising from proactive sourcing will be very different.

- You may be the only candidate being interviewed.
- The interviewer will be 'warm' from the outset. You can even go so far as to say that the interviewer will actually be wanting you to succeed. This contrasts with other kinds of interviews where the interviewer will start from a neutral position.
- There is a chance the interview will end with you being offered the job.

Panel interviews

Some shortlist interviews take the form of panel interviews. The classic panel interview is a structured and formal affair. There will be a chairperson and several panel members, who will each take their turn at putting questions. Panel interviews are normally reserved for very senior appointments.

Some panel interviews are less structured. The panel may be an *ad hoc* body cobbled together for the sole purpose of seeing one shortlist. A typical example is where the board of directors of a company will interview a shortlist of candidates for a senior post. The panel members will be unused to the situation, hence the interviews take some time to get into their stride. The first one will often be a disaster and run way over its allotted time. From the candidate's point of view it will look messy and disorganised.

You won't always be warned if the interview you are going to attend is a panel interview, and it can come as quite a shock to find yourself being ushered into a big room with a table full of people glaring at you. Being prepared for anything when you go for an interview isn't a bad rule of thumb.

Assessment centres

You are only likely to run into assessment centres if you are applying for management or training for management posts with large organisations. Assessment centres are frequently used for graduate intakes.

Assessment centres consist of whole days made up of interviews (one-on-ones), panel interviews, selection tests, presentations and discussion groups (round-table sessions with other candidates). They are usually well organised and may be run 'off site' – at a dedicated conference centre, for example. Assessment centres are sometimes organised by consultants.

4.3 Preparing for interviews

Jane is 23. Shortly after finishing a course in desktop publishing, she applied for a job in the marketing department of a large financial services company. She was pleased to get invited to a preliminary interview and she spent some time researching the company and putting together a portfolio of some of her better work. As part of her preparations she rehearsed a presentation of the material in her portfolio. On the day of the interview Jane arrived early. However, she was kept waiting for 20 minutes, and during this time two other candidates arrived.

The interview was with a Mr Stanley, who signed his letters 'Human Resources Executive'. After Mr Stanley introduced himself and apologised for the late start, Jane asked him if he would like to see her portfolio. He seemed to hesitate before saying yes. Jane then proceeded to go through her material page by page. After about 10 minutes Mr Stanley interrupted her, saying he needed to move on because he had other candidates to see. Jane was taken aback by this. Some of her best work was at the end of the portfolio (intended as a kind of grand finale).

She tried to explain, but Mr Stanley was already going through her application form and firing questions at her. His pace was brisk, to say the least, and on two occasions he actually cut her answers short. At the end he asked Jane if there was anything she wished to know about the job. Jane asked what DTP packages she would be working with. Mr Stanley said he didn't know, then, explaining he had someone else waiting, he brought the interview to a close. He told Jane he would be in touch soon.

Seven days later, Jane got a letter to say she hadn't been successful. She viewed her experience as a bad interview with a bad interviewer – someone who didn't know anything about the job; someone who didn't give her a chance to bring out her best points.

This is an example of interviewer and interviewee on totally different agendas.

What happened here was that the interviewer, Mr Stanley, was running late with his session of preliminary interviews and was struggling hard to catch up. He had probably already said goodbye to his lunch. In came Jane, humping her portfolio and asking him if he would like to have a look at it. Saying no hardly seemed polite and, in fairness to Mr Stanley, he had no way of knowing he was letting himself in for a lengthy and prepared presentation. Also Mr Stanley is a Human Resources Manager. He doesn't know much about DTP, so most of what Jane had to say to him went completely over his head. When he tried to get the interview back on track, he ended up having to rush it.

We can feel sorry for Jane because she is young and quite inexperienced. However, her case study illustrates how planning for interviews can actually go against you if you plan anything which is inconcise, inflexible and incapable of change.

Go to your interviews

Let's start you on your preparations for interviews with the basics – first, getting there. Most people outside the recruitment industry would be surprised to learn just how many candidates fail to turn up for their interview. On the face of it, it is hard to understand why this happens, but our experience of non-attenders is that they fall into one of two categories:

- those who are just unsatisfactory and disorganised;
- those who, for bizarre and irrational reasons, write themselves off before they start. Into this category come people who don't go to interviews when they feel the competition's going to be too stiff ('What chance do I stand?').

Rule number one for interviews is: attend.

Invitations to interviews

You may be invited to an interview by letter, giving you a time and date to attend. Alternatively, you may be asked to phone in to make an appointment. There is an increasing tendency these days for interviews to be arranged over the phone. Managers who have no secretarial support find it far easier to ring people up, and this is why we have given much prominence to availability and in particular to telephone contactability. Candidates who are available on the phone are by and large candidates who get invited to interviews.

What if you find you can't go to an interview? What if the appointment is really inconvenient for you? Ring up straight away and see if you can rearrange it. You will find most employers are only too happy to be accommodating, but don't expect them to be too kindly disposed towards you if you tell them you are only available after 8pm or on Sundays. Be prepared to bend a little. Running out of time-off-work time is a big problem to candidates (loss of availability), hence the importance of all we have said about targeting properly and not squandering your time-off-work time on interviews that are time-wasters. If you really have run out of time-off-work time, then frankly there is not a lot of point in applying for jobs. Give it a break until you can get your availability back.

Finally, on the subject of invitations to interviews, always make a point of confirming that you will be attending. Do this by ringing up and, whenever possible, actually speaking to the person who is going to interview you. There are three reasons for this piece of advice.

- It makes a good early impression.
- It gives you visibility (see Lesson 4, page 154).
- It gives you an opportunity to ask if you can have some information about the company (more on this later).

Remember to keep these conversations short and to the point. Just because you've got the ear of the interviewer doesn't give you licence to start asking a thousand and one questions. If you are too persistent the good early impression you have just made will soon turn sour.

Revisiting your CV

Preparing for interviews is a lot more basic than most people think. The time many candidates devote to psyching themselves up and rehearsing all sorts of weird and wonderful interview techniques would be far better spent re-reading their CVs. This also goes for any other documentation that has been submitted to an employer, such as application forms or letters. Remind yourself exactly what you have said. This is why keeping copies of everything is important.

One of the big mistakes candidates make at interviews is to say something that directly contradicts information they have already given in written form. By re-reading your CV, application form, etc., you can avoid such mistakes.

Another point we have touched on before is to make sure that the CV you are revisiting is the one sent to the employer and not a later version. Discrepancies can occur where several weeks have lapsed between the original application and the interview, or where an agency has arranged the interview and they are holding copies of an old CV.

Planning your diary

One of the most unpredictable things about interviews is their length. At one extreme, they can be over and done with in 15–20 minutes; at the other, they can go on for two or three hours. As a rough rule of thumb, the more senior the job the longer the interview will last. Shortlist interviews will be longer than preliminaries.

Don't make any arrangements which are going to put pressure on you during an interview, such as committing yourself to collecting children or being back at work for a certain time. It may not be your fault if the interviewer is running three-quarters of an hour late, but it won't do much for your chances if you have to excuse yourself halfway through, or if you are sweating to get off and not concentrating on what the interviewer is saying.

Incidentally, interviews running late are not always the fault of the interviewer. Sometimes candidates don't turn up on time, and if there is a procession of interviews this has a knock-on effect on the rest of the day.

Journey planning

Turning up late for an interview is the classic bad start. It strikes an immediate bad impression, which will be very hard to shift.

Think through your journey to an interview and do a dummy run unless it is absolutely impossible (which may be the case if the interview is in another part of the country). Take note of your journey time and any potential hold-ups. If you do your dummy run in the evening, make allowances for daytime traffic. Make allowances too for hold-ups on motorways.

If you intend to travel to the interview by car, check on the parking. Does the employer have parking facilities? Is there alternative on-street parking? A common cause of last-minute hiccups is candidates arriving on time only to find the employer's car park is full. If your interview is in a city centre, or anywhere else which could get congested, a taxi might not be a bad idea – or arrange for someone to drop you off. In planning your journey, always err towards giving yourself plenty of time. There is nothing worse than getting in a last-minute panic because you think you are going to be late.

Researching employers

Finding out more about firms has two functions.

- It enables you to deal with interview questions along the lines of 'How much do you know about us?'
- It enables you to start to form an assessment of the company as a prospective employer.

Here are some hints on how to get hold of information on companies relatively painlessly.

- When you confirm that you will be attending the interview, ask the interviewer to send you some information about the company. This will normally come in the form of some sales literature or a corporate brochure of some description.

- If the company is a public company (denoted by the letters 'plc' after its name), you can get hold of a copy of its latest 'Report and Accounts' quite easily. Simply ring up the Company Secretary's Office and ask them to send you one. It will come free of charge and you won't be asked why you want it. Unless you are an Accountant or similarly trained person you won't make much of the financial mumbo-jumbo, but the 'Chairman's Statement' will make interesting reading. Some sets of 'Report and Accounts' are very glossy affairs, containing all sorts of information.
- Use your network. Do you have friends, relations or other contacts who can give you the low-down on a particular firm? Anecdotal information of this type is quite useful.
- If you have time, check the reference stock in your local library. They usually keep a few trade directories on their shelves.
- Have another look at the advertisement for the job (if it was advertised). Big display ads often contain a lot of information about companies and what they do. This is another reason for keeping ads.
- If you sourced the job via an agency, tap into the agency's knowledge of the employer. This can be a case of not being told anything unless you ask. Sometimes agencies will give you some good nitty-gritty information on firms.
- If a selection consultant (or a head-hunter) is involved, then feel free to tap into this person's knowledge too.
- Does your job give you access to useful information? People who work in credit control or sales, for instance, can get hold of all sorts of information on the creditworthiness of firms.

Revisiting the ad

If you sourced the job from an ad, make sure:

- you keep a copy of the ad;
- you have another look at it before you go to the interview.

The purpose of revisiting ads is twofold.

- They frequently tell you quite a lot about the employer.
- They tell you what the employer is looking for. This will help you when you come onto the next item: reviewing your strong points.

Your strong points

Strong points, you will recall, are the attributes you have which match up to the requirements of the job. Remind yourself of your strong points. Strong points are what you've got to get across at interviews and what will make you stand out from the crowd. It is for this reason they are particularly important at preliminary interviews where the crowd is at its thickest.

Pictures and portfolios

Jane prepared a portfolio of her best work to take along to her interview. Most of us, however, would have a problem with this because our work isn't portable.

Pictures are worth a thousand words, and nowhere more so than at an interview. Photographs of work you have done, or products you have been associated with, avoid the need for long verbal descriptions. This is good for a number of reasons.

- Verbal descriptions are quite hard. Your description may make sense to you, and the interviewer may be nodding along, but the mental pictures forming in the interviewer's head may be far removed from what you are trying to put across.
- When we are talking about our jobs, we can quite easily slip into jargon or technical terminology. A lot of this will go straight over professional interviewers' heads.
- Long verbal descriptions take time, and time is not always on your side, particularly in preliminary interviews.

Pictures, in short, aid your accessibility.

What about portfolios? With certain occupations (design is a good example), taking along some examples of your work will almost be expected. Bear in mind, though, not to overdo it (remember Jane). Select a few examples only. The criterion you should be using is relevance to the job for which you are applying. We appreciate this may mean putting to one side some work you may feel very proud of.

Preparing answers to questions

Every interview is different; every interviewer is different. For this reason, it is impossible to anticipate all the questions you are going to be asked. Three questions, however, come up with such regularity that they are always worth preparing for.

- 'What do you know about us?'
- 'Why are you applying for this job?'
- 'Why do you want to leave?' or, if you are out of work, 'Why did you leave?'

The answers to 'Why are you applying?' and 'Why do you want to leave?' may relate to one another. For example, you may be applying for the job because it offers better pay and prospects. The reason you want to leave your present job may be because it doesn't offer very good pay and prospects.

Let us now look at these three questions in turn and, at the same time, look at what interviewers are fishing for, so you can have the right answers ready.

'What do you know about us?'

Interviewers ask this question for two reasons.

- To see how much pre-interview research you have done, which in turn will be seen as a measure of your interest in the job.
- At some stage in the interview, they will be telling you about the organisation (and the job). They will want to find out how much you know already, so they can decide where to start.

The key to dealing with the question 'What do you know about us?' is to keep your answer concise. Tell the interviewer:

- where your information comes from, i.e. what you have done to find out more about them;

- what you have learned (three or four sentences);
- that it sounds like the kind of organisation you would like to work for.

'Why are you applying for this job?'

Your reply tells interviewers the following.

- Something of your motivation (what makes you tick). This is important because it provides a clue as to how you are likely to perform in certain job situations. For instance, someone applying for a job in commission-only sales needs to be motivated by money. On the other hand, someone with a big money motivation wouldn't be very suitable for a job where concern for others or pride in finished work are the prime considerations.
- Whether the job matches up to what you are looking for. This, if you like, is targeting in reverse or interviewers doing your targeting for you. Their concern, is of course, the same as yours – that the job matches your targeting benchmarks. If it doesn't, then, from everyone's point of view, including theirs, taking matters any further is a complete waste of time.

Again, keep your answer concise. Run through your targeting benchmarks – in essence repeating what you have said in your CV. Say in what ways you feel the job matches up to what you are looking for. You will be referring here to what was said in the ad, or to what the agency has told you, or to what other information you have got on the job (depending on how you sourced it).

Whatever you do, in response to 'Why are you applying for this job?', don't launch off with a long grumble about your present job. However much your grumbling is justified, interviewers are put off by people who come across as moaners (they've probably got enough of them on the payroll already). Don't say 'Because I'm out of work' either. Wanting to get away from something, whether it be unemployment or a bad job with a bad employer, is not in itself a sufficiently strong reason for wanting a job. It conveys the impression that anything will do, which is not what interviewers want to hear.

'Why do you want to leave?'

The reasons for the interviewer asking this question are much the same as the reasons for asking you why you are applying for the job.

- The answer tells the interviewer something about your motivation.
- The answer exposes any mismatches. If, as an example, your reason for wanting to leave is to escape from a requirement to work away from home, and if the job you are applying for has a similar requirement, then quite clearly there is little point in proceeding any further. Of course, in an ideal world, a mismatch such as this would have become apparent well before the interview. Your CV would have flagged up that you don't want to work away and the employer would have picked it up. You would not have been asked to the interview.

Again, your answer to 'Why do you want to leave?' needs to be concise and to avoid grumbling. Here, to illustrate the point, are a few wrong and right ways of saying the same thing.

Wrong	**Right**
My boss expects me to work for peanuts.	I think my skills might be better rewarded elsewhere.
I'm in a dead-end job with a dead-end firm.	I'm looking to join a progressive organisation where if I work hard, I can hope to have better prospects.
They don't encourage you to go for training. They're not interested.	I want a job where I can advance my career with good training opportunities.
My boss has never heard of please and thank you.	I would like to work for a more professionally managed organisation.

As you will see, the trick in each case is to turn the negative into the positive and to focus attention on where you want to go rather than the problems of where you are now.

• WARNING •

While on the subject of acceptable and unacceptable answers, there are some things you should never say when you are asked why you want to leave a job.
- 'They expect you to do the impossible.'
- 'They expect you to work overtime at the drop of a hat.'
- 'They expect you to do everything.'
- 'They go round giving out their orders . . .'

Unfortunately, in the UK there is a long history of people or groups of people arguing about who does what, or what they consider or don't consider to be their job. Flexibility is a big issue these days, particularly with smaller employers and with employers who have to fight their corners in fiercely competitive markets. In consequence, there is an expectation that people will be willing to put in extra hours if that's what's needed. There is an expectation, too, that people will be willing to jump to and stand on their heads if necessary. Alarm bells will ring if candidates come across as inflexible.

If you are out of work, the question 'Why do you want to leave?' will be substituted by 'Why did you leave?' Redundancy is now the main reason why people find themselves on the dole. The job went because markets shrank or because the firm reorganised or because new technology came along and reduced the need for people. This is the essence of redundancy: an event over which the individual has no control.

Giving 'redundancy' as the reason why you left the last job may not, however, satisfy some interviewers. They will want to know more. There are two reasons for this.
- In some organisations selection for redundancy is based totally or in part on job performance (as opposed to last in, first out), hence a prospective employer may be keen to establish that your selection for redundancy was not because you were a poor attender, or because you did not do your job very well.

- The term redundancy is used by some candidates as a cover-all. You find people saying they have been made redundant when they have in fact been dismissed for misconduct. This happens in many cases not because the candidates concerned are trying to obscure the truth but because they genuinely believe that the term redundancy covers any loss-of-job situation.

If you give redundancy as the reason why you left your last job, you must further qualify this information by stating:

- what brought the redundancy about, e.g. factory closure;
- how many people were made redundant, i.e. it wasn't just you;
- why you were selected, e.g. last in, first out, or because you did a job for which there was no longer a requirement.

But what if your reason for leaving the last job wasn't redundancy? What if you did get the sack because you did something wrong? Or what if you handed in your notice because you felt you couldn't take any more? What do you say when you are asked why you left?

Our advice, in all situations, is to tell the truth. With interviewers, truthfulness is a definite winning point. Employers in general can cope with people who lack in experience or who need chivvying up from time to time, but they can't cope with people who tell lies. Once suspicion that the candidate is not telling the truth has entered the interviewer's mind, then the closing signals start to flash. Honesty, on the other hand, and particularly disarming honesty, can be a way of turning a bad point into a good point.

Finally, in preparing answers to 'Why are you applying for this job?' and 'Why did you leave?', make sure that what you plan to say is consistent with what you've put in your CV or on the employer's application form.

'Are you subject to any restraint clauses?'

This is a question increasingly asked at interviews. It is most frequently levelled at candidates:

- for top jobs;

- who are in sales, or in jobs with a high degree of customer contact;
- who are in employment in which they have access to confidential information;
- who are employed in creative or inventive roles.

Contractual restraints are being used increasingly to protect businesses against the activities of ex-employees. For instance, it would be highly damaging to a company to have its customers lured away by a former Sales Manager who is now working for a competitor. Not only will this person know who the customers are, but there is also knowledge of pricing structures to take into account. Restraint clauses are inserted into terms and conditions of employment to prevent employees wreaking damage on businesses they leave.

At an interview, you may be asked if you are subject to any contractual restraints; so, before you go, check:

- your terms and conditions of employment;
- your original job offer or letter of appointment;
- any letters you have subsequently received concerning your employment and the conditions attached to it (if you have been promoted, or if your job has changed in any other way, then check any letters you received at the time this happened);
- your service agreement (if you have one).

If you find you are subject to a restraint clause, take a photocopy of it and put in the bundle of documents you take to the interview. If you get asked a question, you can produce it.

Preparing questions

When you go to an interview you will want to ask some questions about the job. Asking questions has two functions.

- You may get offered the job. If so, you will have to decide whether to accept it or not. You need facts on which to base this decision.
- Asking questions, like doing research, demonstrates to the interviewer that you have a serious interest in the job.

Confine your questions to important issues, notably the following.

- Pay and when pay is reviewed. Where part of the pay is subject to results (bonuses, commissions, etc.), establish how much is basic and guaranteed and how much has to be earned. Senior managers and professionals would not normally expect to be paid for additional hours, but for jobs lower down the ladder it pays to find out if payment is made for overtime and if the overtime payments are subject to premium rates.
- Company cars (where relevant). What kind are they and how often are they changed? What contribution (if any) will you have to make towards the running? For example, do you have to pay for the petrol you use privately?
- Hours of work.
- Pension provision – does the company operate a pension scheme? If so, how much will you contribute? On what is your final pension based? (They may have a booklet which you can take away with you.)
- Private medical schemes (e.g. BUPA, PPP). Does the company provide cover? If so, does the employee have to contribute anything? Are there any arrangements for the employee's family?
- The main responsibilities of the job, i.e. what you will be doing. If any of it is unfamiliar territory to you, then what arrangements will there be for training?
- To whom you report (who will be your boss).
- Would employment be subject to a trial or probationary period? If so, how long is this period?
- If prospects figure in your targeting benchmarks, what are they? If you do well, what kind of advancement can you expect to look forward to?
- If the job involves travel, living away from home or unusual conditions, what allowances and expenses are paid?
- Why is there a vacancy? The job may be a new job, but if not it will be interesting to learn why the last person left.

The point of these questions is that you need to know the answers to make like-for-like comparisons with:

- your present job (if you have one);
- your targeting benchmarks.

If you are offered the job, your decision on whether to accept or not will rest largely on these comparisons (more on this in Chapter 5, where we will look at job offers).

There are lots more questions you may want to ask, but before including them on your list ask yourself the following.

- Are they really that important?
- Will they send out the wrong signals to the interviewer? Arrangements for payment during periods of sickness may be an important concern. Will you be paid your normal wage or will you be put on statutory sick pay (SSP)? If the former, is there a cut-off point after so many weeks? If you ask too many questions about sick pay, however, an interviewer might start to get the impression that you are the kind of person who has a lot of time off work.

Jot your list of questions down on a notepad, leaving spaces for the answers. You will be taking this notepad to the interview, so make sure it is presentable. Planning your interview questions and making a note of them is important. Otherwise you will find you forget to ask them, and you won't get another chance.

4.4 Going to interviews

What to take with you

Keep your 'going to an interview' kit to a minimum, so as to avoid:

- being burdened down;
- looking for something during the interview and not being able to find it.

You will need to take the following items.

- The letter inviting you to the interview (if you had one). You may need to produce it when you arrive (to a Security Officer, for example).
- Your notepad containing your questions, and a pen or pencil.
- Your pictures (see page 125).
- Any letters of reference you have from previous employers and any relevant certificates, e.g. those which will confirm qualifications relevant to the job. (Take these just in case you are asked for them. It will save having to send them in later.)
- A copy of your CV (see why on page 137).
- Your driving licence (if you have one).
- For non-EU nationals, your work permit.
- Sufficient small change to enable you to make phone calls (this is in case you get delayed) or to put in a meter in a car park.
- The employer's telephone number (again in case you get delayed).
- A newspaper (not a tabloid!) to read.
- If it looks like rain and you're not going by car, an umbrella. Arriving wet and bedraggled won't do much for you on the first-impressions front.

Arriving on time

Even if you arrive early, don't present yourself at the employer's reception until ten minutes before your interview. We say this for three reasons.

- The comfort factor: reception areas are not always conducive to long waits – especially in small firms. They may consist of little more than cold, dark vestibules. Seating isn't necessarily guaranteed!
- With preliminary interviews, you may bump into the candidate with the interview before you. There is potential for minor embarrassments which, on the whole, are best avoided.
- You may be in the way and end up feeling a nuisance.

What if you are late? It can happen: modern traffic conditions are very unpredictable, especially on motorways, and travelling by public transport can just as easily be subject to delays. The very minute you know you've got a problem look for a phone. Ring in and ask to speak to the interviewer. If the interviewer is not available, then ask to be put through to someone who can take a message (the telephonist will probably offer to do this for you). The gist of what you are saying is that you have been delayed (give the reason) and that you are going to arrive late (give an estimate of how late). Ringing in is a case of 'if in doubt, do it'. In fact, the earlier you do it the better. Thinking you might just make it is usually inviting catastrophe.

What to wear

Once it was an unwritten rule of interviews that you went along in your Sunday best. Now candidates are less sure. Interviews and interviewers are extremely unpredictable, and for this reason it is still best to play safe. Avoid casual clothes. You may feel awkward in your nice suit if the person interviewing you is wearing jeans and trainers, but you will feel even more awkward if the positions are reversed.

The clothes you choose to wear for an interview should be:

- smart;
- clean;
- a reflection of you.

The last is important. The great thing about humanity is its diversity. We are all unique, and our uniqueness (individuality) has a key part to play in how successful we are at getting jobs.

We have seen already how homespun CVs – the way they are put together, the words people use – project something of the candidate in a way in which bland, expert-prepared CVs don't. We have seen how employers latch onto these bits of colour and how the engagement factors start to work. The same applies to dress. The way you dress is part of your uniqueness – a very visible part. The colours and styles you prefer and the way you put items of clothing together all convey something of you which employers (interviewers) notice and can and will latch onto.

Clothes have two other functions which play a part in the chemistry of interviews.

- They are an early impression (perhaps the very first).
- They are a recollection point. Interviewers will often remember candidates by what they wore at the interview (the girl in the blue dress, the bloke with the floral-pattern tie, etc.).

Here are a few useful tips on dressing for interviews.

- Stick to simple styles and colours. Remember that everyone has different ideas about what looks nice, and something simple is more likely to get universal approval.
- Avoid wearing too much jewellery, for the same reasons.
- Clothes should be clean and freshly pressed.
- Clean your shoes (interviewers still look at candidates' shoes!).
- Don't keep your clothes where they may pick up nasty smells.
- For men, shirts with the top button undone and ties that hang loose are a definite turn-off.
- Beware the dreaded anorak! Candidates arrive for interviews, find it is raining and slip on the awful anorak which lives on the back seat of the car. The chances are the awful anorak doesn't get washed too often, so it will smell to high heaven the minute it becomes wet. Then there's the problem of what to do with it when you arrive at to the interview. An umbrella is much better.

Certain items of clothing are definitely out:

- trainers;
- jeans;
- track suits/shell suits.

Grooming

Wash your hair before you go to an interview and use a good-quality deodorant. Needless to say, greasy hair or nasty odours won't get you very far on the early-impressions fronts. Also avoid strong-smelling deodorants, perfumes and after-shaves. Evidence of a recent haircut is a plus point. Even long hair will benefit from a trim.

Long waits

You may be in for a long wait when you go for an interview – particularly a preliminary interview. This is why it's a good idea to take a newspaper with you.

Being asked to fill in an application form

When we talked about application forms we warned you that they can be presented to you at any point, and it is not uncommon for candidates to be asked to fill in an application form when they arrive for an interview. This can be the cause of much head-scratching, particularly when trying to remember dates. You can avoid this by having your CV with you.

Travelling expenses

Some companies reimburse an interviewee's travelling expenses. This is more likely to happen where the interviewee has had to travel a long way.

Sometimes you will be told in the letter inviting you to the interview that travelling expenses will be reimbursed. Sometimes you won't. Sometimes the interviewer will ask you at the start of the interview how much you have spent on travel, and some companies will require you to fill in an expenses-claim form.

Don't expect to have your travel expenses reimbursed, even for long journeys. Some firms take the view that getting to interviews is your problem, not theirs. This can sometimes leave candidates who are short of funds in a bit of a dilemma.

If no mention of travelling expenses is made in your invitation to the interview, and if you can't meet the cost out of your own pocket, then it is advisable to ring up and check if the company reimburses expenses before you go. If the answer is no, then clearly you have to choose between cancelling the interview or somehow getting the money together. Don't leave it until you arrive to ask whether the company pays travel expenses or not. If the answer is no, it's too late anyway (you've spent the money), and you also run the risk of starting the interview off on a bad foot.

• WARNING •

PUTTING YOUR BILL IN AFTERWARDS

Some candidates have adopted the practice of waiting for the turn-down letter to drop on the doormat before sending in their bill for travel expenses and other costs incurred in attending the interviews. The common form of such demands is curt, and the reason for sending them has probably more to do with pique than hardship. Letters such as these seldom get the response the candidate is hoping for. The unfortunate part, though, is that the candidate undoes at a stroke any good he or she has done. 'So what?' some candidates will say, feeling judgement has already been passed on them, so what have they got to lose?

So what? So it will be a pity if unbeknown to them they happened to be the number-two choice and the number-one choice decides to turn the job down. It will be a pity, too, if another equally interesting opportunity happens to arise in a few weeks' time and the company – before advertising – decides to revisit previous candidates.

4.5 Preliminary interviews

In many ways, these are the hardest interviews to handle. There are four reasons for saying this.

- You will be one of many. The competition is at its most intense. To get on to the next stage (the shortlist), you will need to stand out from the crowd.
- The time allocated to you will be limited.

- Interviewers doing one interview after another tend to get tired and switch off.

- The interviewer may be a Human Resources Manager or a Selection Consultant who has been hired in specially to do the preliminary interviews. These people are generalists: they won't know too much about the work you do.

Strategy for preliminary interviews

Your accessibility is the big issue here. What you say about yourself at preliminary interviews needs to be capable of being understood, and being understood first time. Here are a few points for you to consider. Some of these we have touched on already, but it will do no harm to repeat them.

- Keep your answers to questions short and concise. Don't rabbit on. As a rule of thumb, the more you say: the less clear it becomes; the greater the chance the interviewer will switch off and stop listening (watch for those glazing-over eyes); the more you are wasting precious interview time.

- Not all regional accents are clearly understood (interviewers from the south of England seem to have the most trouble). If you have a strong regional accent which the interviewer doesn't share, try to speak slowly. The same is true if English isn't your native tongue. This is not incidentally an invitation to talk with a 'plum in your mouth'. Nothing sounds worse.

- Consistent with shortness and conciseness, don't get into too much detail with your answers. Bear in mind that anything technical or steeped in jargon will go straight over the heads of interviewers such as consultants or human resources specialists. So much the better if you can use pictures to overcome the need for long or technically complex descriptions.

- Listen to questions – don't do the politician's trick of answering a different question to the one you've been asked.

- Don't take over interviews – don't, like Jane, launch off into long speeches or presentations. The penalty here is that time will run out, and important points (important to you) will not have been covered.

'Tell me a bit about yourself'

This is the kind of opener which throws candidates into a spin, so be ready for it and don't treat it as an invitation to launch off into a ten-minute, watered-down, oral version of your CV. If you do, you will be wasting precious interview time. Concentrate instead on getting across your strong points and keep the details to a minimum.

Success at preliminary interviews

Candidates who are successful at preliminary interviews are candidates who pass through the 'broad suitability' test. There are two main facets to 'broad suitability'.

- Candidates must be capable of doing the job or doing the job after an acceptable period of training.
- Candidates must be seen as the kind of people who will 'fit in'.

The judgement as to who will and who won't fit in can be based on very narrow and largely subjective opinions of 'the way things are here' or 'the way we work'. For example: 'In this firm we have to work very long hours. We don't employ young married people because they soon get fed up.' Call these prejudices if you like, but many of the preconceived views on who is and who isn't likely to succeed in a job are based on employers' past experiences with people. Where held, these views are of course something over which candidates have no control. Neither will candidates have any knowledge that these requirements exist. The 'hidden criteria', as we call them, are very much a feature of employment in small successful firms, which form such a significant part of the modern market that they are worth knowing about. Otherwise well-qualified candidates who are baffled as to why they didn't get put on shortlists may well find that the answer lies in one of these hidden criteria.

4.6 Interviewers' questions

Every interview is different. Every interviewer is different. Consequently, the range of questions you can get asked at an interview is endless. We are now going to look at questions which, in one form or another, come up regularly. We will examine these questions under broad subject headings and, at the same time, have a look at what interviewers are trying to discover about you.

Where you live

Questions likely to be asked on this subject are as follows.

- How far away is your home? Can you get to work reasonably easily? Do you have a car, or is there public transport? Could the journey become a problem to you in the future? For example, what would happen if you no longer had access to a car? Of concern to employers are people who take on quite difficult journeys to work (because they need the job), then find that the daily routine gets too much for them (the onset of winter is usually the trigger-point). Short-stayers in jobs are costly to employers, particularly if training has been given.

- How long have you lived at this address? If you have not lived at this address very long, then where did you live before and again for how long? Employers are understandably concerned about the stability of people they are considering for employment.

- Do you own the property, or is it rented? Home ownership and the financial commitment that go with it (mortgage, etc.) are a compulsion to work. On the other hand, if the employer wants you to relocate, home ownership could be viewed as a drawback.

Your marital status

Questions asked at interviews can extend to spouses' or partners' occupations. One of the concerns here is that spouses and partners should not be involved in competing or conflicting lines of work. Also, jobs that involve long or peculiar hours, long-distance travel or long periods away from home can conflict with the demands of permanent relationships.

Your health

This is of immediate concern to employers, because health is inextricably linked to your attendance at work. Poor attenders are a big problem for employers. They are an even bigger problem for small employers where there are fewer pairs of hands to cover for staff who are ill. Expect questions about your health, even if you have put on your CV (or on any application form you have filled in) that your health is good. Expect to be asked in some detail about your attendance record in your present or last job. A typical question would be 'How many days have you been away sick in the last 12 months?'

Here the advice is to answer the question honestly. Employers aren't looking for 100 per cent attendance records (most of us succumb to the 'flu now and then). They will have more problems from a credibility point of view with candidates who claim they never have time off.

Your driving licence

You may be asked to produce your driving licence, particularly if the job involves travel, and more particularly if the job involves the use of a company vehicle. This is why we advised you always to put your driving licence into your going-to-interviews kit. On the other hand, you may simply be asked how long you have been driving and if you've clocked up any endorsements. Don't try to explain away endorsements ('It was a bit of bad luck the policeman was standing round the corner'). Employers are not impressed with people who make excuses.

Your family background

What your parents do (or did) for a living holds an interest for employers. If you had to battle through to university from a deprived inner-city background, it says a lot for your grit and tenacity. If your father was in the army and you spent most of your childhood abroad, this suggests that you wouldn't have too many problems fitting into an overseas posting.

Your education

Young people (under-25s) are more likely to face detailed questions about their education, simply because it forms the most significant part of their lives. Questions about education recede as you get older. Work experience will start to assume greater importance for interviewers.

Examination achievements appear in your CV or on any application forms you have filled in, but don't be surprised if interviewers start asking you about examinations you have failed. They are not trying to get at you (most people have failed an exam at some point in their lives). Rather they are trying to build up a complete picture of what you have done, what have you achieved and – in a academic terms – where your strengths and weaknesses lie. Candidates don't tend to list failed exams in CVs and applications forms and this is why some interviewers ask about them.

Your employment history

For most people this will form the greater part of any interview – questions about the jobs you have done and why you left them. Apart from getting a clear understanding of the range of your experience, employers will be trying to pick up clues from your reasons for leaving as to:

- what makes you tick;
- how much you will put up with;
- whether you have failed in any of the jobs you have done (an indication you could fail again).

As part of your interview preparations we suggested you had an answer ready for one of the questions 'Why do you want to leave (your present job)?' or 'Why did you leave' (your last job)?' We warned you about giving negative answers to these questions ('My boss is an idiot'), and this piece of advice extends to reasons for leaving previous jobs. We also warned you that redundancy as a reason doesn't stand up on its own: it requires explanation and clarification (why you were selected).

Employers appreciate that people leave jobs for money reasons, but they start to get concerned when money reasons keep cropping up again and again, particularly if the periods spent in jobs are very short. The impression is that the candidate in front of them is someone who is perpetually shopping round. Interviewer: 'Why did you leave Bloggs and Co.?' You: 'Because Boggis and Co. offered me more money.' Fine, but was this because you applied to Boggis and Co. or did they approach you? If it was the latter, then it would be best to say. It dispels the impression that you spend your spare time going after better-paid jobs.

A question mark could also be put over a candidate who cites 'improved prospects' as the reason for moving jobs, when the new job doesn't seem all that different to the old one, i.e. it doesn't make sense. If, as so many people do, you saw moving sideways as the eventual means to moving upwards, then this would be worth explaining to the interviewer.

Here is one final piece of advice on dealing with questions about your job history: when you refer to previous employers, talk about 'we' and 'us' rather than 'they' and 'them', e.g. 'We got a British Standards kitemark in 1992'. It then sounds as if you were part of the team rather than a bystander.

Your interests

Some interviewers will ask you what you like to get up to when you are not at work. The conventional view of questions about out-of-work activities is that employers consider it to be good thing for staff to have ways of relaxing and taking their minds off work. However, total commitment and long hours are very much the bywords of successful modern firms, and the view that is taken of absorbing hobbies and achievements in sport has changed in the last 20 years.

Take care these days if you are asked questions about what you do in your spare time.

- Don't put yourself across as someone who is obsessed by a hobby or other out-of-work activity. If conflict with the job arises, then employers will want to feel sure that they've got someone who is going to put work first.

- Don't start laying down conditions to employers. (Interviewer: 'We can get pretty busy, especially in the summer months. Everyone has to put in long hours. Would this give you any problem?' Candidate: 'No; not unless it was Wednesday night, when I go to my ballroom-dancing class.')
- Be aware that employers won't be impressed by dangerous pastimes that might result in injuries and time off work.
- Don't give a great long list of hobbies. The interviewer will begin to wonder how you manage to fit work in.
- Keep your answers to questions about hobbies short. It wastes valuable interview time and, unless the interviewer happens to share your interests, you will find he or she switches off.
- Be especially careful of any of the above if you are long-term unemployed. You can give the impression of being someone who has got out of the work habit; someone who has developed a pleasant lifestyle centred around fishing or going off in the caravan; someone who would find the rigours and disciplines of going back to a job intrusive and a severe shock to the system. Employers have had bad experiences with the work ethics of long-term unemployed people.

Questions interviewers don't ask

As we have seen already, one of the features of the modern market is that managers often handle their own recruitment, as opposed to getting a professional to do it for them. This includes doing their own interviewing. In these situations, how good the interviewing is depends on:

- how much experience the managers have had;
- how much time they give to it.

Some interviews are awful and the candidates concerned are justified in feeling short-changed. Just about everyone who has been active on the job market in the last 15 years has had at least one bad interview experience.

Bad interviews, however, don't necessarily mean that the jobs are bad or that the firms are bad employers. The manager who makes a hash of an interview may turn out to be an excellent person to work for.

In the modern market, candidates need to develop some failsafe systems to take account of poor interviewers or interviewers who don't give their interviews enough time. This is all part of that vital principle of keeping control. Inexperienced interviewers and interviewers who are in a rush frequently omit to ask all the questions they need to ask. They get half the story, and then move on.

In this next little scenario, the candidate is being interviewed for a job as a Production Engineer. Unbeknown to the candidate (it wasn't mentioned in the ad), one of the requirements of the job is a thorough knowledge of being able to program machine tools using software made by a company called Fanuc.

> **Interviewer**: 'I want to come onto your programming skills. You have been with Bispham and Bloop for two years now; can you tell me what software you use?'
> **Candidate**: 'Mainly GE.'
> **Interviewer**: 'What about Fanuc?'
> **Candidate**: 'Not a lot – we've recently bought a lathe with Fanuc controls but I haven't been involved with it very much.'
>
> * * * * * * *
>
> **Interviewer**: 'What about your previous job at Bodgitt Brothers?'
> **Candidate**: 'That was nearly all Fanuc. I did all the machine-shop programming for about six and a half years.'

The significance of the dotted line in the script is that this is where some interviewers would end the interrogation. The view they would form as a result is that the candidate hasn't had a lot of experience with Fanuc – which is entirely wrong.

The trick here is to spot the line of questioning ('There must be a reason why I'm being asked about Fanuc') and keep control – tell the interviewer about the experience with Bodgitt Brothers. Another kind of question that doesn't get asked is the one that doesn't seem to need asking.

> Corinne is an Architectural Technician. She is applying for a job as a Site Engineer with a company making components for the building industry. The job involves visiting sites throughout the UK and advising contractors on the correct methods of fixing the company's products. Some of these visits involve long trips and nights away from home. The job is a good job with a good salary and a company car – which Corinne doesn't have at the moment. Corinne is married with two children (aged 4 and 8). Her husband, John, has a heart condition. He was pensioned off from his job with the local authority two years ago, and since then he and Corinne have swapped traditional roles. He acts as house-husband and looks after the kids while she goes out and earns the bread and butter. The arrangement works well. Apart from anything else, Corinne has the better earning power – John, even when he was fully fit, was only qualified to do manual jobs.
>
> Corinne's interview is with the company's Contracts Director, a Mr Walsh. The interview goes well. Most of Mr Walsh's questions are about Corinne's experience and he seems more than satisfied with the answers she gives. Her domestic arrangements are not brought up, and the interview ends on a upbeat note with Mr Walsh saying she stands a good chance of getting on the shortlist. Understandably Corinne is disappointed when two weeks later she gets a letter from Mr Walsh saying she hasn't been successful.

Mr Walsh didn't shortlist Corinne because he saw from her CV that she had two young children. Since the job involved living out of a suitcase three or four days a week, there was, to him, a very obvious point of conflict. He saw no reason to ask further questions.

Whether knowing about Corinne's role swap would have cleared up Mr Walsh's misgivings entirely is another question; but she would clearly have stood a much better chance of getting the job if this information had been imparted.

Part of the principle of keeping control is accepting responsibility for what information flows from you to the interviewer. Corinne – and this, we appreciate, isn't very easy – should have spotted the conflict between being a mother of two young children and a job which involves nights away from home. She has an answer, yes, but it is her responsibility to make sure this answer gets across. In short, she has got to get it into the interview at some point that John is not only entirely happy to be fulfilling the traditional woman's role but that he has been doing it for some time, i.e. it works.

Other questions that don't get asked at interviews are questions which might cause the interviewer some difficulty or embarrassment. Inexperienced interviewers often don't like asking questions which have the appearance of prying. Take the example of Zeke, who has lived with Sally for eight years and, because of complications at Sally's end, they have never got married. On his CV, Zeke has put that he is single with three children ranging in ages between 18 months and five years. This is perfectly true, but to an employer it could mean one of four situations.

- (a) A divorced man with custody of three young children.
- (b) A divorced man whose wife has custody of the children.
- (c) A single man living on a permanent basis with a woman with whom he has fathered three children.
- (d) A divorced man living on a permanent basis with a woman with whom he has fathered some children, while others are by a previous relationship.

Zeke's situation is (c). (a) is the situation is which is most likely to bother employers. (What happens when the kids are sick? What happens when overtime or unusual hours are required?) Zeke may have a problem with interviewers who find it awkward to ask personal questions. They might say nothing and think Zeke is, or might be, in category (a).

The need to make pre-emptive strikes, answering the questions interviewers don't ask, tends to relate to the requirements of the job. Corinne's situation would not have been so critical if, for example, she had been applying for a nine-to-five position in an office.

What sort of situation calls for pre-emptive strikes?

- Any domestic situation outside the normal.
- If you have moved home a number of times.
- If you have had a lot of jobs in a short space of time.
- If you have been dismissed.
- If you have been made redundant.
- Any downwards or sideways moves in your career.
- If you have suffered from any medical complaints (both past and present).
- Anything else about you that is unusual or that a prospective employer might consider an impediment.

4.7 Closing interviews

Did your strong points come across?

An interview will run its natural course, and you should allow this to happen. Apart from answering the questions you are asked, and watching out for those critical questions you aren't asked, your main concern in keeping control of the interview is to make sure your strong points are coming across. Nine times out of ten this won't require any input from you. The interviewer's questions will provide you with the natural opportunity to say what you need to say.

If you sense the interview is going to close before you have managed to bring in one of your strong points, then this is the signal to hit the emergency button and say something like: 'Oh, by the way, I noticed in your ad you mentioned that experience with a such-and-such would be helpful. I used one of these when I was at Bloggs and Co. I thought I ought to tell you.'

Finding out about the job

In most interviews, the interviewer will set some time aside to tell you about the job and to deal with any questions you may have. 'What do you know about us?' is often used as the lead-in to this part of the interview. Once you have dealt with 'What do you know about us?' along the lines suggested on page 126, the interviewer will probably fill in the gaps in your knowledge and then tell you a bit more about the firm and the job. Here is where you get your notepad out and start ticking off the points on your list of questions.

Should you ask if it is OK to make notes? Our advice is yes – not that we could think of any possible objection. It just seems more polite.

When the interviewer has finished, you will probably get an opportunity to ask questions. Go though your list carefully. You should find that some, if not most, of your questions have already been answered.

Don't ask questions:

- about trivial things that will have no bearing on your overall view of the job;
- about things the interviewer has already covered (it shows you haven't been listening);
- that give the wrong impression and set off warning bells, such as 'How many days am I allowed off sick?'

What happens now?

We have now reached the end of the interview, and this is where we go back once more to keeping control: getting the information to keep control as the selection process moves on.

If the interview is a preliminary interview, then the next stage will be the selection of a shortlist. You are going to need to know the following information.

- When you will be told if you are on the shortlist or not (a very rough idea).

- How this information will be communicated to you: by letter or by phone, or would it be better for you to ring in? If you can engineer it, the last of these three options is highly desirable from both keeping-control and visibility points of view. Be warned, though, that not all interviewers will like the idea of candidates phoning them up. If you sense resistance to the suggestion, back off.

- If you've been recommended for the job by an agency, will the interviewer be coming back direct to you or through the agency (so you know who to chase)?

- Whether any dates have been pencilled in for the second interviews (so you can plan your availability).

- Who will be doing the second interviews.

- Whether or not there is a starting date for the job. With most jobs – particularly replacements for staff who have left or who are leaving – the starting date will largely be determined by the successful candidate's period of notice. Some jobs, however, have fixed starting dates. An example is where there is an intention to take on a number of people for the same job (e.g. graduate intake or a company recruiting a team of service personnel). The need for a common starting date will arise because some kind of induction training is being planned. If there is a fixed starting date, it pays to know well in advance – again, so you can plan your availability (no holidays, etc.).

Make a note of the information you are given in response to your questions; otherwise you will forget.

If you are going on holiday during the period when second interviews are due to come up, or if anything else could conflict with your availability, then make sure you tell the interviewer. There are plenty of instances of candidates who have been put on shortlists but who finished up in the limbo file because when it came to it they couldn't be contacted.

If your interview is a second interview, it is going to be useful for you to know when you are likely to hear the result and, again, how it will be communicated to you (by letter or phone).

Don't expect to get a decision at the end of an interview. It certainly won't happen if the interview is a preliminary. Don't do what some schools of thought on the subject of interviews recommend – that is to ask the interviewer if you've got the job. There is absolutely no point, and you run the risk of ending the interview with an embarrassed silence (not a good end impression!).

'Is there anything you would like to add?'

This is a question that sometimes gets thrown in at the end of interviews and sets candidates off scratching their heads for something to say.

Take the view that if you've succeeded in registering all your strong points during the course of the interview then you won't be wanting to add anything except for your closing statement (see below). Don't feel you need to fill the space created by this question with superfluous and irrelevant information or information which the interviewer has already heard. It is quite easy to put the kiss of death on an interview in the closing moments and undo all the good work you have done by waffling on about nothing (and may be putting your foot in it at the same time). Unless you've got something really important to add (like a strong point which hasn't been brought out), you will do far better by keeping quiet.

Closing statement (wanting the job)

Sometimes at the end of an interview an interviewer will ask you if you are interested in the job. Irrespective of whether you are asked this question or not, it is important to close off interviews by saying that you want the job and that you believe you can do it. This is known as your closing statement.

End impressions

There are two critical moments in any interview. The first, which we have discussed already, is at the beginning. This is when the halo effects form. The second is at the end. End impressions are important because these are the impressions interviewers carry forward. Ideally, your first impressions and your end impressions will be consistent.

A *faux pas* on the part of the candidate made in the middle of an interview will have:

- a chance to correct itself;
- a chance of being overlooked because of a good early impression (the halo effect).

A *faux pas* made at the end of the interview will:

- stay fresh in the memory.
- occur at the point in the interview furthest removed from the good early impression, i.e. when the halo effect is at its weakest.

4.8 After interviews

'How did I do?'

After an interview, this is the first thing candidates tend to ask themselves.

The single most striking thing about self-assessment of interview performance is how often candidates get it wrong. We put this to the test a few years ago. We took a sample of candidates who all thought they had put in a good performance at interview, and asked the interviewers concerned for some feedback. In over 75 per cent of the cases the feedback was poor. What does this demonstrate, apart from the utter pointlessness of trying to guess at the outcome of interviews?

- Candidates tend to judge interviews by how well they got on with the interviewer. Their optimism is based on nothing more than feeling they hit it off with the person who sat on the other side of the desk. Good interviewers are, of course, good at putting candidates at their ease, and this is all part of the technique. In short, their friendliness gives no clue whatsoever to the way they are thinking.

- Some interviewers will actually make encouraging remarks to candidates – even to the point of suggesting that they stand a good chance of being offered the job. Always take remarks like with this with a pinch of salt. The interviewers concerned are usually inexperienced and make remarks like this to everyone.

- Candidates often judge interviews by their length. They take a long interview as a good sign, and vice versa. This can be true to an extent. Busy interviewers don't waste time on people. But there is the problem that what to one interviewer is a long interview will be a short one to another, i.e. the length of the interview is more a question of the interviewer's style.

- Candidates feel they have done well if they have demonstrated that they can do the job. They forget there are other factors involved in selection, such as whether they would 'fit in', and the large number of other candidates who are equally competent. This is where candidates can end up getting disgruntled. 'I could have done the job with my eyes closed', you will hear them say when they get the 'No thank you' letter. They end up blaming the interviewer.

The danger for you in reading interviews favourably is that you automatically build up expectations. This isn't good, because disappointment and the anger that goes with disappointment are what lead to discouragement. As we have seen already, you won't survive in the modern market if you allow yourself to become discouraged in any way. Take special heed if you happen to be unemployed.

After you have been for an interview, it is quite natural to think about it; but, as far as you can, leave it at that. Don't be optimistic or pessimistic – view the outcome as something that could go either way.

> **LESSON 4** Visibility
>
> Part jokingly and part cynically, it has been suggested that success these days has more to do with being in the right place at the right time than suitability for the job. There is, however, an element of truth in this observation – and being in the right place at the right time is what we call visibility.
>
> Cold calling is based on visibility: phoning up and presenting

yourself at the right time. The facts that you are there, you are visible and you offer a solution can get you the job.

Busy employers, employers with no help to hand (i.e. typical modern market employers) will be those who are most susceptible to visibility.

Another form of visible candidate is the temp. Temps are there, working in the firm already. We will be looking at temping and at visibility in Chapter 6.

Visibility can play a part further on in the selection process, too. Selected candidates don't always accept the offers made to them – putting the recruiter back to square one – or almost. The thought of having to start all over again (and re-advertising the job) will be particularly unappealing. Hence the first reaction is to revisit the shortlist. Was there an acceptable number two?

If this happens, all well and good, but employers don't always do the obvious. The reasons are as follows.

- It doesn't occur to them.
- They've already turned the number-two choice down, and they find it too hard to go back.
- The number-two choice knows he or she is the number-two choice, and some employers will feel this is a bad start.
- They assume the number-two choice won't be interested – because of being turned down or because of the passage of time.

If you've come close to getting a job (e.g. been on a shortlist), then you can occasionally reap benefits from putting yourself back in the frame, making yourself visible again. Obviously the timing of this is critical. Here is what you must do.

- When you get the 'No thank you' letter, count off five working days, then write the firm a polite letter saying how disappointed you were to hear you didn't get the job but thanking them for the interview and expressing your continuing interest should any similar opportunity arise again. The point of this exercise is that you will be the most visible alternative candidate if the number-one choice has turned the job down.
- Ring the company up in about a month's time. Remind them who you are (this is important) and ask if they managed to fill the

job. Explain you rang on the off-chance they were still looking for someone: you were very interested in the job and disappointed you didn't get it, etc. The important thing again is that you have re-established your visibility – this time to coincide with one of two possible events:

– the selected candidate didn't start, and they're flapping round deciding what to do next;

– the selected candidate has started, but it has already become apparent that they made the wrong choice. Again, they will be flapping round wondering what to do about it.

If you got your 'No thank you' letter via an agency, you need have no compunction about ringing up the recruitment consultant you dealt with and saying you want to be put straight back in the running if the job should happen to come back on the market.

Post-interview availability

If an interview has gone favourably, you will either be required to attend a further interview (shortlist) or you will be offered the job.

We can quote plenty of cases of candidates who missed out on second interviews and job offers simply because they couldn't be contacted. We can quote the case of Mr B who was offered a good job, a job he desperately needed because he was unemployed. The offer came in the form of a letter which lay on Mr B's doormat for nearly a fortnight because Mr B, without telling anyone, had decided to take advantage of a spell of good weather and go off with Mrs B in their caravan. The letter asked Mr B to phone the company concerned to confirm that he would be accepting the offer and to agree a date of starting. When they got no response from Mr B, the company's Personnel Officer rang him and left a message on his answering machine. The message asked him to make contact urgently. The Personnel Officer did this twice. Finally, because they had no information to the contrary, the company concluded Mr B wasn't interested in the job and offered it to someone else.

Predictably, Mr B was very upset when he got back and learned what had happened but, interestingly enough, he attached none of the blame to himself. In his view, it was the company's fault for wanting to do things in such a big rush.

Whatever we may think about Mr B, there is one lesson to be learned from his experience: the modern market won't waste time on people. It won't put up with ditherers and it won't make allowances for candidates who aren't available. Apart from anything else, employers have had too many bad experiences with people – particularly people who don't respond to job offers.

Ensuring your availability by rearranging holidays at short notice isn't always easy. Deposits may be at risk, and there may be other difficulties too. Family holidays may be tied to school holidays. Holidays may have to fit in with people you work with, and so on. But, if another interview is looming or if a final decision on a job is imminent at around about the time you are due to go on holiday, then the first thing you need to do is to tell the interviewer at the interview.

Even so, you are still relying on the interviewer to record this information, and some warning signals should start to flash if you don't see the interviewer writing it down. It is a good idea (always) to have someone check your post and answering machine when you are away on holiday – if your going-away happens to coincide with one of these critical moments. Give the person some method of contacting you, e.g. the phone/fax number of where you are staying. Failing this, ring in every three or four days.

Allowing interviewers to put you off

This is worth mentioning, because a lot of candidates allow themselves to be put off by their experiences at interviews. Being kept waiting a long time; being left in a draughty corridor for ages; being given the 'third degree' by a bad-tempered interviewer; being confronted by an interviewer who doesn't seem to know anything about the job – these are the kind of things that cause candidates to have second thoughts about pursuing their applications any further.

Don't expect the modern market to be nice to you, because it won't. Standing round in draughty corridors and muddled interviews are pretty much the norm now. Not allowing this sort of treatment to get to you is all part of application.

4.9 Having interviews and being turned down

First, let's take a look at why candidates fail at interview and what, if anything, they can learn from the experience.

Not getting onto shortlists

Trying to pinpoint the reasons for lack of success at interviews is extremely difficult. There is always the x-factor, of course: the interviewer simply didn't like you. There is the other x-factor, too: the hidden criteria – the quirky ways in which firms view themselves and which you can do nothing about.

Rule number one is: never attempt to draw conclusions from the experiences of one interview. Let's use the example of Ann (a real case).

Ann went for an interview and got turned down. The interview was arranged by an agency, so Ann was able to get some feedback from the Recruitment Consultant involved. The interviewer, she learned, didn't feel she had enough drive and ambition for the job, and the Recruitment Consultant suggested Ann should work on this. At the next interview she went to, she made a point of saying all sorts of things about where she wanted to see herself in five years' time. Again she got turned down. This time, the feedback via the agency was that the interviewer felt her expectations were too high.

However, if you are consistently failing preliminary interviews, which means you don't get onto shortlists, this can mean one of a number of things.

- The first thing to examine always is your accessibility – in particular, are you getting your strong points across? Go through what we had to say on pages 97–98. If you are satisfied with your accessibility, ask yourself if your strong points really are just that – and remember that 'strong points' means 'strong points regarding a particular job'. If, for example, you are plugging the same set of strong points at every interview, then this is a clue that you are going wrong.

- You are applying for jobs you can't do. In theory, you shouldn't have been at the interview in the first place, but because employers' procedures aren't perfect no-hopers can slip through.

- You are making a poor early impression. Something is happening in the first few minutes of your interviews which is putting interviewers off – something you don't know about. If your interviews are short, if you sense interviewers are 'going through the motions', if they don't make notes – these are all little indicators that you are making poor early impressions. Don't rack your brains over this: the reasons for poor early impressions are usually pretty basic.

- Equally, your end impressions could be at fault. Are you, for instance, guilty of going off into long rambles when you are asked if there is anything you want to add (sometimes known as 'talking yourself out of the job')?

- Are you shooting your credibility in the foot with discrepancies between what you are saying and what appears on your CV/application form?

- Without meaning to, are you coming across as a know-all ('done it all/seen it all')? The corollary of knowing it all is not being the kind of person who is prepared to learn or to adapt to new circumstances.

- Are you falling into the trap of using your interviews as a kind of therapy: to have a good old moan about your present job and/or your boss? Interviewers, particularly the professionals, give the appearance of being sympathetic listeners, but really what they are doing is silently writing you off.

- Are you doing what Jane did earlier – taking interviews over and cutting across the interviewer's efforts to keep the interview on track? Are your interviews failing because they don't run the course?

Getting onto shortlists, then getting turned down

If this is happening to you regularly, it indicates that you are passing the test of broad suitability but failing on the finer points.

Feeling you have failed because your interviews don't turn into jobs is a mistake. For example, if you are getting onto shortlists for jobs which have had exposure on the visible market (advertised), you are doing well. You can take it that there has been a lot of competition – particularly if the job is a good job – and you can pat yourself on the back for managing to get into the last three or four. All you need to do now is keep going. Sooner or later you will land the job you want. The main danger for you is reading the signs wrongly, and changing your approach. Don't.

Failing with proactively sourced interviews

What about jobs you sourced proactively, and where you are being interviewed without competition? How do you view failure in these situations? Here, quite different rules apply. If you are getting interviews from your proactive sourcing, and if you are getting consistently turned down, then something is wrong. The interviewer should be wanting you to be suitable, for all the reasons we have mentioned, and the misgiving he/she has must be pretty fundamental, because saying no to you probably means having to go through the hassle of a full-blown recruitment exercise.

Before you go jumping to too many conclusions, though, be careful that:

- you are not judging your efforts on a small number of interviews (under five) where interviewers' quirks and hidden criteria might be the explanation for your lack of success
- the turn-downs really are turn-downs. Proactive sourcing sometimes exposes situations where firms are only thinking about recruiting.

A final word

Don't expect to be offered every job you go for. Success every time is probably a bad sign (under-targeting). A further indication of under-targeting is if you are regularly going to interviews and getting offered jobs but find yourself turning them down because they don't measure up.

Summary

A great deal has been said and written on the subject of interviews and not all of it is relevant to modern conditions. Indeed, the chances of you ever attending a classic textbook interview are becoming increasingly remote. We have warned you about judging companies by their competence at interviewing. Small to medium-sized firms have become an increasingly important provider of quality jobs, but by and large they rank as poor performers when it comes to interviews. Larger firms divide into two distinct types.

- The fragmented, decentralised, de-layered, flattened-down or hollowed-out companies, where the constituent parts will be in precisely the same boat as the small to medium-sizers.

- The firms that can support a Personnel or Human Resources Department with professional interviewers on tap, or who will fork out the necessary expenditure to hire in the services of Selection Consultants. Here is where you might encounter the classic interview.

The diversity of interviewing styles makes it very difficult to give candidates advice that will hold good in all situations. What will find favour with one interviewer will be regarded as a flawed performance by another – and so on. Given this general unpredictability, we have suggested in this chapter that you base your interview stratagems on a two-part analysis.

- First, what kind of interview is it? In particular, is it a preliminary interview where you will be one of a number of candidates and where limited time will be available for you to get your strong points across? We have stressed that with preliminary interviews you need to remember that you are being assessed against a test of 'broad suitability'. The interviewer will be looking for a shortlist, not for someone to whom to offer the job. Accessibility has a key part to play in your approach to preliminary interviews, and we have made a number of suggestions on how you can enhance your accessibility – notably in the conciseness of your replies and statements.

- Second, what kind of interviewer is interviewing you? Is he or she a professional – a Selection Consultant or an in-house Human Resources Manager who has had formal training in interviewing? On the other hand, is he or she one of the growing number of managers whose lot in life seems to consist of doing more and more work with less and less help? With the latter especially, we have alerted you to the need to make pre-emptive strikes at 'the questions they don't ask'.

In all of this arises the question: just what is it that interviewers are looking for these days? What qualities do they seek in people? To many candidates, this remains a complete and utter mystery. They go to interviews for jobs they can do blindfolded and then get turned down without a hint or an explanation. Baffled, they either blame the interviewer for his or her lack of competence, or they blame the interview for being too short. Alternatively, they take the view that the firm didn't know what it was looking for in the first place.

We have encouraged you not to read too much into the outcome of interviews. They are highly subjective (one person's view of another) and subject to all manner of quirks and prejudices – what we have referred to as the 'hidden criteria'. You can't do anything about hidden criteria. You won't even know they exist. Because of hidden criteria, the fact you could do the job while bound in chains and performing a pirouette won't have a lot to do with the eventual outcome of the interview.

Another facet of selection is that firms these days err on the cautious side – they are unwilling to take chances with people. This is partly due to employment-protection legislation and the difficulty of getting rid of people who prove to be a problem. It is also partly due to the potential disruption factor – the effect on other employees – of people who don't pull their weight or who grouse or who are liable to take time off unnecessarily.

Interviewers are very vigilant to the possibility of introducing a rotten apple into the barrel, so candidates need to be careful what they are saying at interviews. A chance remark is often all it takes. Be very careful, in particular, about the reasons you give for leaving jobs or for wanting to leave your present job. For example, 'My boss makes unreasonable demands on me' could mean either 'My boss *does* make unreasonable demands on me' or 'I'm difficult and awkward and I don't like being given orders'. The play-safe interviewer will always conclude the latter.

Finally, on the subject of interviews, here is a word about trying to be super-slick, because you feel this will enhance your chances. It won't. When you go to an interview, be yourself. Somewhere along the line someone has got to take a shine to you. The engagement factors have got to work, and at the end of the day people are going to like you for what you are, not what you are pretending to be. Apart from anything else, you stand a reasonable chance of making a good job of being yourself.

Questions and answers

Preparing for interviews –'I'm subject to a restraint clause'

Q *About six years ago I became a director of a company (a small, wholly-owned subsidiary of a large group), so in real terms the directorship meant very little to me, apart from a few extra perks. Part of the deal at the time was that I went onto the standard group service agreement.*

The group has just announced that the company is to close. As you can imagine, this news came as a severe blow. Still, I thought I had been quite fortunate when two days after the announcement I received a phone call from the Managing Director of a rival business offering me a job on more or less the same terms. I mentioned my good fortune to a colleague who completely took the wind out of my sails by saying I couldn't take the job because of a clause in my service agreement preventing me from working for any competitor for three years! I looked it out straight away and found to my dismay that he was right.

I haven't accepted the job offer yet, but as you can imagine I am in an absolute quandary as to what to do. I have spent the last 28 years in the same trade, so if you take competitors out of the frame I am practically unemployable. I am now beginning to think myself foolish for signing the service agreement in the first place. There again, I didn't anticipate I was going to be in this position.

A Don't despair, all is not lost. Speak to your boss straight away and explain the situation you are in. Most companies who put people on restraint clauses don't have enforced redundancy in mind. Does the closure of the subsidiary mean that the group will no longer be active in this particular market? If so, you going to a competitor can't possibly do them any harm, and hence there is no reason why they shouldn't be able to release you from the restraint. You can probably get a verbal OK on this pretty quickly, and exchange letters on it later on. But don't let the job offer slip through your fingers. Don't leave any deathly silences either – tell the MD of your competitor exactly what's going on. Tell him you'll find a way of taking the job come hell or high water!

If for any reason the group decides to hold you to your restraints, then take advice from a solicitor. The restraint is probably not enforceable anyway. As you quite rightly say, it renders you unemployable (no court of law would support this) and it may in any event be unreasonable (three years is a bit steep).

Getting across to interviewers – are regional accents a disadvantage?

Q *I am a Liverpudlian and people tell me my accent goes against me in interviews. Is this true?'*

A By the law of averages, there will be some interviewers somewhere who don't like Scouse (Liverpool) accents. Equally, there will be some interviewers somewhere who don't like

Glasgow or Brummie (Birmingham) accents. This is the nature of selection: at the end of the day, it is one person's view of another and as such it is subject to all manner of quirks and prejudices.

The biggest problem with regional accents is that some of them are not capable of being understood. Unfamiliar accents cause the biggest problems. If you have an accent that is commonly used on television or radio, it will not be so much of a problem.

Given that you can be understood, a regional accent can be a plus point. It gives you that bit of individuality which is so important and which interviewers latch on to (an engagement factor). One of the worst things you can do at interviews is to try to affect a posh voice.

Interviewers' questions

Q *I am 36 (female) and married with no children. Ten years ago – when I was last applying for jobs – I got sick and tired of interviewers asking me whether I intended to start a family. They don't seem to ask this question any more. Is everyone suddenly much more enlightened, or are they worried they might get done for sex discrimination? On the other hand, perhaps they think I'm past it!*

A Is there more enlightenment about? Perhaps there is, but judging by the remarks we hear (uttered privately, of course) some employers are still pretty paranoid about young women who might get pregnant. The statutory time-off provisions and return-to-work rights are those aspects which worry them most. Whether they admit it or not, small busy firms, which make up so much of the modern market, find these things hardest to cope with.

You are suggesting that 'Are you planning to start a family?' could have become one of those dreaded questions employers don't ask and which you as a candidate need to pre-empt. The trouble with statements like 'We're not planning to have a family for at least five years' is, first, they are pretty meaningless and, second, they might raise a concern which wasn't there in the first place.

So we would say no; don't deliver a pre-emptive strike every time you go for an interview just because you happen to be a woman of child-bearing age. If an employer has really got a hard-and-fast view on the subject of young women in key jobs, then nothing you say is going to shift it anyway. Sadly, it is one of those hidden criteria you can't do anything about. On the other hand, would you want to work for people like that anyway?

FIVE

GETTING JOBS

5.1 Offers of employment

Congratulations, you've got the job. Someone may ring to tell you, but the chances are the good news will reach you in the form a written offer of employment to which you will be asked to respond.

> Sean has been offered (by letter) a job with a firm which competes with his present employer. Sean's main reason for putting himself on the market is money, and the competitor has offered him £2,000 a year more. For this reason, Sean has every intention of accepting. Sean goes along to see his boss and shows him the letter. His boss is very perturbed and asks Sean if he will stay if the money on offer can be matched. Sean says yes, and his boss says he will speak to the Managing Director.
>
> A week goes by with no word. Sean corners his boss again. This time his boss tells him that he has spoken to the Managing Director, but the best offer they can come up with is another £500 a year. Sean explains this isn't enough and writes his notice out there and then.
>
> When he gets home Sean writes a letter accepting the job, and posts it next day.
>
> Three days later, Sean gets a letter back from his prospective new employers. It informs him that his acceptance has arrived too late and the job has now been offered to someone else.

Sean can't be accused of trying to use the competitor's offer to secure a pay rise for himself – the suggestion to hang fire came from his boss. But what he wasn't aware of was the void he was creating: the complete absence of communication between him and his prospective employers. Because of this void, they assumed Sean wasn't interested in what they had to offer and, like many employers, they have got used to people who don't bother to reply. Some firms would have sent out a warning shot before actually withdrawing the offer ('If we don't hear from you by . . . ', etc.), but there is certainly no guarantee this will happen.

Sean, of course, lost control. What he should have done was ring up whoever signed the offer of employment after the first conversation with his boss. Clearly he needed to buy himself a bit of time. He needed first of all to say 'Thank you' for the offer of employment (very important), and to indicate his high level of interest. He needed to explain why he needed a few days to think things over (big decision, etc.). But, most importantly, he needed to keep control: to say when (the precise date) he was going to get back to them with his answer. In this context, Sean would need to appreciate that the length of time to think things over needs to be proportionate to the task, i.e. it doesn't take three weeks to think over a good job offer. A further extension to this aspect of keeping control is to apply the same deadlines to his boss ('I have to let them know no later than . . . '). This in turn will serve to focus his boss's mind on the task of pinning down the Managing Director.

Personnel handbooks

Some offers of employment (particularly those made by larger firms) are accompanied by handbooks of various descriptions, giving details of standard terms and conditions of employment and company rules.

In such cases, the actual offer letter may be quite brief and refer you to the handbook for the details. The information in the letter will probably be confined to the non-standard aspects of the package, notably the pay, the job title, to whom you will be responsible, the starting arrangements, etc. If there are any special conditions that apply to you, or if there is anything in the handbook that doesn't apply to you, then the letter will normally draw your attention to it.

Sometimes, but not always, the offer will be accompanied by a job description. Some companies believe in job descriptions and some don't. Some will give an outline job description or summary of the main duties and responsibilities within the body of the offer letter.

If there is a pension scheme, you may also get a copy of the members' handbook. Other documents may also be enclosed with your offer of employment. For instance, if the job involves a company car there may be a separate set of rules covering the terms of its usage.

5.2 Deciding to accept or decline

You have now reached the point where you have got to decide whether to accept an offer of employment that has been made to you, or whether to turn it down.

Getting the information you need

Sometimes interviews don't go as planned. Sometimes you don't get a chance to ask all the questions you want to ask. Either the interviewer is in too much of a hurry, or you forget something. For all sorts of reasons you can find yourself in receipt of a job offer when you are still short on vital facts.

Never accept a job until you have all the information you need; but, before you think about ringing up, make sure that what you want to know isn't detailed in the small print of your job offer or in any documents accompanying it. Another point to bear in mind before ringing up is to ensure that you are not descending into the trivial. It may be useful to you if the firm will cash a cheque for you on Fridays to save you stopping off at the cashpoint, but it won't be the end of the world if they don't.

If you feel you really must phone to find something out, how should you handle such fact-finding phone calls?

- Make them straight away. Speak to the person who made you the offer.
- Remember to show your appreciation – say how very pleased you are to have been offered the job. Say 'Thank you'.
- If you haven't had a handbook, ask if there is one and, if so, keep control by asking if you can pop in and pick it up.
- If there is a specific point you want to clear up, ask first of all if it is covered in the handbook.
- Make a note of anything you are told.
- If you are now happy to accept the job, say so. Say that you will be confirming in writing within the next few days. Again, keep control.
- If something you have been told gives you cause for second thoughts, buy yourself a bit of time by saying 'Thank you' and that you'll be getting back to them shortly. Say when (control).

Just as bad as accepting jobs when you have only half the facts is turning them down in the same situation. There are candidates who, just because something isn't spelt out to them, assume the worst. ('It doesn't say they pay you for overtime, so that must mean they don't.') Often, of course, this is just an excuse for 'I can't be bothered to find out'.

> **LESSON 5** Using your instincts
>
> This is another essential tool of career power. Instincts are something that nature provides us with. We all have them. They are conditioned into us from childhood, and they are there to ensure our survival.
>
> Listen to your instincts, therefore, and learn to trust them. They can be the best help there is when it comes to knowing which jobs to take and which to leave alone.
>
> Job situations, at the end of the day, consist of people and your instincts will tell you a lot about people. Instincts rarely let you down.

Weighing up offers

The first thing to appreciate is that there is no such thing as the perfect job. Every job has its good features and its bad features. What you need to assess is how the good and bad balance up.

Let's take the example of Alan. Alan is in a job where he gets free lunches. He views not getting free lunches as a bad feature in any job he is looking at. As most of us know, not many firms give their employees free lunches, so Alan, without appreciating it, is taking a jaundiced view of most of the job market.

In weighing up offers of employment, candidates have a habit of applying the 'topping up on what I've got' approach. They want every item of the job package matched or bettered, plus whatever it is they have been looking for. They are prepared to concede nothing, and are surprised to find that none of the jobs they are offered seems to come up to scratch.

One such example was Debbie. Debbie worked for a firm where holiday entitlement built up with service. She had been with the firm nine years and she had accumulated 4 extra days' holiday on top of the standard 25, giving 29 in total. The jobs she was being offered had holiday entitlements ranging, in the main, from 22 to 26 days. In some cases, the firms had provision for service days, but as a new starter Debbie didn't qualify for these. Debbie's view of her job offers was that she was being asked to give up some of her holidays.

This 'topping up on what I've got' approach doesn't work in the modern market. Employers and employment conditions are so diverse that you are unlikely to find many point-for-point matches. There are always going to be plus and minus factors, so when you weigh up job offers you need to adopt a broader, more flexible approach. It also pays to remind yourself just what you are doing on the market in the first place (back to your targeting). Debbie, for instance, was looking to improve her prospects in a more dynamic organisation. Some of the jobs she was offered were with firms that fitted this description very nicely (high-growth companies in modern industries with expanding markets), yet still she chose to turn the offers down. Even to this day (she is still looking), she doesn't see that she has done anything particularly wrong.

The net result of applying such harsh tests to offers of employment is that you end up turning them all down. Really, you are back to searching for something that doesn't exist, or something that is so scarce it is going to take a long time to find – and more than likely you never will, because discouragement sets in first.

Another very important question to ask yourself when you are weighing up job offers is to what extent you are suffering from cold feet. Putting yourself on the job market can be great therapy. If the boss has been vile to you one day, or if you didn't get the pay rise you expected, shooting off a few job applications makes you feel better. The buzz that goes with making applications persists through to the interview stage. You start to get a bit of your self-esteem back, and being selected for the shortlist really puts a spring in your stride.

Then you get offered the job, and all of a sudden it's make-your-mind-up time. Things no longer look quite so clear-cut. You find you've never really contemplated leaving, not properly. It means saying goodbye to friends, saying goodbye to old familiar surroundings, and taking the long, lonely walk into the unknown.

At this point, a lot of candidates crumble. They turn the job offer down, giving an invented reason. The truth for them is that they should never have been on the market in the first place. Sadly, they had to get to this stage to find this out.

Whether getting a job and turning it down does you any good or not (therapeutically speaking) is a matter for conjecture. What is certain is that it is something you shouldn't keep doing.

Avoiding bad moves

Deciding whether to take a job or not is a decision which is taken partly on the available facts and partly on instinctive feelings, which you develop as you go through the various stages of the selection process. Any job move involves risk, but the thing to remember about risk – any kind of risk – is that it has an up-side and a down-side.

The up-side is getting whatever it is you are aspiring to, whether it be more pay, better prospects, a job nearer home or one with less tortuous hours, and so on. You achieve your aim and in most cases this is the happy outcome. Down-sides are admittedly pretty frightening. A bad move means at best unhappiness and at worst failure (you quitting or getting the sack). In today's climate, the likelihood of the latter is much greater than it used to be.

So what can you do to avoid bad moves? What can you do to minimise the down-side risk in taking another job? Here are a few tips.

- Watch out for situations where you apply for one job and end up being offered another. This happens more often than you may think. The difficulty here is that some part of the selection process has been spent on an entirely different agenda. You need to 'wind back' and, in particular, make sure you've got all the information you need on the second job, and that it conforms to your targeting benchmarks.

- Beware any situation where you sense you are being 'sold' a job. All jobs have snags and a healthy sign is where the employer is telling you about the snags.

- Beware especially of employers who make promises to you – the bigger the promises the greater the need for caution. Promises of future pay increases call for particular scrutiny.

- Beware of anything that seems vague or imprecise. (Candidate: 'When will my pay next be reviewed?' Employer: 'We'll have to see.')

- Beware employers who won't put anything in writing to you.

- Pick up on the kind of employers who give themselves let-outs. An example is the kind of job offer that is made conditional on the retention of a contract or the business of a specified customer. Any employer faced with the loss of a substantial part of the order book has to contemplate laying off staff. So why draw attention to the fact in an offer of employment? Frequently, the answer is that the loss of the contract or the customers' business is in the offing. The threats have already been made. In short, there is a little more to this than normal commercial risk.

- Read the small print in your job offer and in any accompanying documentation. Things are not always as they seem, so make absolutely sure (beyond all doubt) that you are being offered a permanent job. So many jobs these days are temporary, or 'temp to perm', or fixed-term, or some other convolution, that you need to be especially careful. (A surprising number of people have made the mistake of giving up a permanent job for something that turned out to be temporary. Usually, they only have themselves to blame.)

- Beware jobs where the pay figure quoted incorporates overtime earnings or performance-related elements, e.g. bonuses or commissions. There is nothing wrong with earnings derived in this way, providing the employer isn't trying to conceal the true picture from you.

- Watch out for culture clashes. Big-company people frequently find it hard to fit into small, entrepreneurially managed firms where the decisions all emanate from one person (the owner).

- Read what we have to say about enticement (see page 189). Accepting the 'offer you can't refuse' can sometimes be a grave mistake.

Trial periods

Reference to trial or probationary periods in job offers can make you feel jittery, but in real terms trial periods are pretty meaningless. Even if a firm doesn't have a stated trial period, it doesn't mean they'll hold back if you fail to perform. So don't let trial periods put you off. You could find yourself turning down perfectly good job offers needlessly.

References

Job offers are sometimes conditional on one or more satisfactory references being received. Firms sometimes stipulate who the referee(s) should be, e.g. someone acquainted with your work or someone who can vouch for your character.

References don't normally cause problems, because the referees are nominated by you; and you wouldn't be putting forward the name of anyone who is going to say bad things about you. Don't hand your notice in, though, until the references have been cleared. This may call for some control on your part, such as phoning the firm up to see if they have had the references and if they are OK.

Some firms will want you to organise the references. Others will prefer to do this themselves (they may have a specific form they want the referees to complete). Some firms will prefer to take up references verbally (over the phone).

Medicals

If the offer of employment is conditional on a medical, then don't hand your notice in until you know that the results of the medical are satisfactory.

Service agreements

The offer of a senior management or professional job in a large company could contain a stipulation to enter into a service agreement. A service agreement is a legal covenant which binds two parties: the employer and the employee. It sets out the terms under which the employee agrees to serve, yet really it is very little more than a glorified set of terms and conditions of employment.

Service agreements are normally confined to senior management grades. Frequently they contain such things as:

- restraints on what the employee may or may not do in the event of leaving;
- specific expectations of people at this level, in terms of loyalty, the use of confidential information, acting at all times in the best interests of the company, etc.;
- top job perks.

Candidates who are new to service agreements can find them intimidating. They are written in 'legalese', and they have to be signed and witnessed. Small wonder, therefore, that many people receiving them for the first time rush off to their solicitors for advice.

One of the difficulties with service agreements is that they are standard documents that companies dish out to everyone at or above a certain level. It is unlikely, therefore, that a company will be keen to make alterations or delete sections just to accommodate one particular person, particularly a newcomer.

The message to candidates who are confronted with service agreements for the first time is not to view them automatically with suspicion. By all means talk to a solicitor if it makes you feel more comfortable, but use the advice you get selectively and intelligently. Solicitors are apt to raise snags that are unlikely to happen and wouldn't be earth-shattering if they did.

Feeding a long list of small gripes back to an employer without comment and prefaced by a remark such as 'This is what my solicitor says . . . ' runs the risk of being interpreted as a refusal to sign – and, therefore, that you don't want to take the job.

Restraint clauses

The appearance of a restraint clause in an offer of employment or a service agreement can be a cause for concern. The commonest form of restraint is the one that stops you joining competitors. Often, too, the restraint will extend to businesses associated with competitors, and the phrase 'serve in any capacity' will be used to stop ex-employees using their knowledge to benefit competitors in the guise of a supplier, e.g. a self-employed consultant.

To be legally effective, restraints need to be limited:

- in terms of time – the period in which the restraint is in force will start from the date of leaving and will need to run for a specified number of months/years;
- geographically – for instance, to within a defined radius of the company's main operating base or within certain defined countries or trading zones.

No court of law would entertain a restraint clause that is too wide or that goes beyond what is reasonable to protect a business. For instance, a clause restraining an ex-employee from joining a competitor anywhere in the world would be viewed as unreasonable if the company concerned only traded in the UK. Similarly, a restraint clause which prevents an ex-employee from earning a living would also be viewed as unreasonable.

This leads us to the interesting fact that the more draconian a restraint clause happens to be then the less likely it is to be enforceable.

Restraints can apply in other directions, too. For example, it is quite common for companies to put restraints on the use of confidential information.

Refusing to enter into any restraint agreement because you view it as an infringement of your liberties may be a fine stance, but it could also remove a large slice of the available market from your grasp. If you apply for senior jobs, restraints will be something you have to put up with.

Contractual periods of notice

> Grant took a top management job with a firm of estate agents. At first, the firm stipulated a 12-month period of notice linked to a service agreement, but Grant demurred. To use his words, going into a new job was bit like contemplating marriage. They needed a period of living-together first – with no strings attached. In the end, Grant settled for the service agreement with its 12-month notice period coming into effect after two years. Up to then the notice period would stand at two months on either side. Grant reasoned that if he didn't take a shine to his new employers he wouldn't have the problem of having to go back on the market with a 12-month-notice millstone hanging round his neck.

We wish Grant well in his new job and hope he never has cause to rue his decision to opt for a short notice period.

In any job the riskiest period is at the start. You don't know them, they don't know you, and all sorts of things can happen.

Getting the short, sharp exit treatment is a risk for all of us. We are then left with the task of getting the best possible deal for ourselves, and often the only bargaining tool we have is our contractual period of notice. The short, sharp exit means we won't have been given notice (or not much anyway), so the question of compensation for the contractual breach arises.

Settlement of contracts is a subject all on its own. If it happens to you, then the best advice is to seek the help of a good lawyer – by which we mean a lawyer who has had experience in this field. So commonplace are employment-related disputes now that most large law practices carry a specialist.

The point here, though, is that the best lawyer in the world won't be able to do much for you if you've done as Grant did and settled for a short period of notice. So don't view long notice periods as a bad thing, and don't turn jobs down because of them – or, like Grant, seek to negotiate them down.

5.3 Accepting job offers

You've decided to accept the job; now you need to let your new employers know.

Acceptance letters and further voice contact

With Sean, we saw the difficulties of not responding to job offers quickly enough. When you receive a job offer, you need to act on it straight away. Phone up the person who sent it to you and say:

- 'Thank you' and how pleased you are;
- that you will be accepting;
- when you hope to start;
- that you will be confirming this in writing within the next few days.

These actions on your part not only dispel any doubt, but they also start off a new round of first impressions: the first impressions of you, the new employee.

Some offers of employment come with a form or a tear-off acceptance slip for you to complete and return. Alternatively, there may be an extra copy of the offer letter for you to sign. In these instances, include a short covering letter to say how pleased you are to accept and how you are looking forward to starting.

Take a photocopy of your acceptance, then send it by recorded delivery. Two days later, phone up the firm to make sure they've got it. The point of this further voice contact will emerge a little later on.

Starting arrangements

There are a number of things you need to know about starting. Some of these points will have already been explained to you either at the interviews or in the offer of employment. This little checklist should help.

- Check your starting time on the first morning. This may be different to your normal starting time to take account of induction procedures.
- Check to whom, and where, you should report.
- Check what to bring with you (P45 form; details of your bank account; any special clothing or equipment, etc.).
- If a company vehicle is involved, check any arrangements for its collection.

If you are in need of any information about starting arrangements, you should ask when you ring in with your confirmation of acceptance.

Handing in your notice

This is the point of no return, the point at which some candidates start to get cold feet.

Your starting date in your new job will either be fixed (a date given to you) or it will be determined by the length of notice you have to give. With fixed start dates, you may not have to hand in your notice straight away. For example, if your start date is in three months' time and you are only subject to one month's notice, then you can delay handing in your notice for two months. The golden rule is: don't hand your notice in any earlier than you have to.

You have had two recent bits of voice contact with your new employer: first when you confirmed your acceptance; and second when you rang in to see if your acceptance letter had been received. The point of these voice contacts is that, if your new employer is contemplating a U-turn for any reason, then you will be giving yourself a chance of picking up the warning signs. Put the other way round, you will have had very recent confirmation that the firm's intentions are still the same. You can feel reasonably reassured that no unexpected development has reared its ugly head and you are as safe to hand in your notice as you can be.

Next, you are going to leave your present employment on good terms (more on this subject later), so:

- ask to see your boss, i.e. don't just hand over a letter or put it in the internal post;
- express suitable regret and that this is a decision you have reached only after very careful consideration;
- don't be furtive – tell your boss where you are going (unless for any reason you have been asked to keep this information secret);
- identify the date on which you intend to leave (consistent with your notice requirements) – this will expose any difference of opinion between your boss and you on what period of notice you should serve;
- discuss things that 'need to be done', e.g. project work that needs to be completed or work that will need to be handed over to someone else;
- say that you will be confirming your notice in writing.

Straight after this meeting, put a letter together confirming your notice and the date on which you will be leaving. Make sure you date this letter, and keep a copy. Find a few kind words to say, too. Here is a good example.

> Dear Bob
> After much heart-searching I have decided to accept an offer of employment with the Grimbolts Group. This means I will be leaving Sprockets on 24 July. The last ten years have been very rewarding from my point of view and I would like to express my thanks and appreciation to you personally for the help and support you have always provided. I will take many treasured memories with me.
> Yours sincerely

Being persuaded to stay

This subject is worth dealing with because it happens a lot. In highly competitive industries, the loss of a key member of staff to a rival could spell danger or even disaster. Employees will therefore be bought off (given what they want) simply to prevent them leaving.

Allowing yourself to be bought off has a head and a tail to it. On one side of the coin, you will be staying with the devil you know. The other side of the coin is the nagging feeling that you've forced their hand, and why didn't they do it before?

Firms tend to get over having their arm twisted behind their backs, but a real area of concern with pay buy-offs is – what future progress are you going to make on the salary front? If they've hiked your salary up by £2,000 to stop you leaving, then surely they're now going to view you as overpaid. What happens when the next pay review comes up? The answer is to wait for the next pay review, but don't be too surprised if you find yourself getting less than you thought.

The bottom line in these situations is that you must be prepared to go back on the market again in the not-too-distant future.

5.4 Turning jobs down

This is the other eventuality – deciding not to take the job you've been offered.

We have already been through some of the reasons why

candidates turn jobs down. We have pointed to the problem of making impossible comparisons. We have looked at candidates who get cold feet. But if you keep turning jobs down it suggests you are going wrong somewhere.

The first port of call has to be your targeting. Are you targeting the right kind of jobs in the first place? A common problem is that candidates wander off their targets over a period of time. Call it 'target drift', if you like. Fine-tuning targets in the light of interview experience is highly desirable, but occasionally it can lead people into diluting their targeting (because of their lack of success); they then find that when they get offered jobs these don't measure up. Just be aware of this potential difficulty, and put it right if you have to.

Don't expect every job to be the 'offer you can't refuse'. Again, the diversity of the market comes into play – there will always be jobs with hidden snags to them, snags that don't become apparent until you get the offer in your hand. Similarly, there will always be jobs your instincts warn you off.

Renegotiating an offer

Before you turn the offer down, is it worth going back to the firm concerned and seeking to renegotiate any of the terms into something more to your liking? Bear in mind that firms won't be prepared to negotiate terms that are standard to all or a number of employees. Working hours, restraint clauses and the choice of company cars all probably fall into this category.

Usually, however, the subject for renegotiation is pay. You are offered the job but the figure put forward falls below your targeting benchmark. If the choice is between turning the offer down and seeking to renegotiate a term which has a chance of being flexible, then you are clearly losing nothing by giving it a try. Be clear, though, that renegotiation is a route of no return. Once you have said that some items aren't to your liking, then it is hard to go back on your words at a later stage.

How do you set about renegotiating some term or terms in a job offer?

- Many employers will baulk if they feel someone is trying to twist their arm, so it is best not to give the impression that you are trying to negotiate. Let the suggestions come from them.
- As with acceptances, act quickly if you are seeking to renegotiate.
- Phone in and speak to the person who offered you the job.
- Identify the reason for calling, i.e. that you have had the job offer (say 'Thank you') and that, yes, it was very pleasing but regrettably the salary was about £2,000 less than the figure you had in mind, and for that reason *only* you have had to decide to decline. What a pity (etc.) because in all other respects the job seemed exactly the kind of opportunity you were looking for. In short, make it perfectly clear that there is one problem and one problem only.
- Shut up when you have said this. Don't ruin things by suggesting solutions ('If only something could be done about the pay . . . ').

There are three possible outcomes here.

- A big silence, in which case don't worry because you have sown the seed. End the conversation. They'll be back to you if the seed germinates.
- You'll be asked some kind of 'What if?' question such as: 'What if we met your figure; would you accept then?' Be ready to say yes. Be ready to ask for it in writing.
- They'll tell you they can't increase the offer – end of story.

Saying no in writing

Except where you are seeking to renegotiate a term or terms in an offer, it is easiest to turn jobs down by letter. A rejection letter need only be brief. You don't have to go into reasons, but don't delay, and remember to say 'Thank you' for the job offer.

The point of making a graceful exit from offers of employment is that next week the same firm may be advertising something which may be much more to your liking and you need to feel you can go back.

Turning down jobs sourced via agencies

Agencies that work on results (which is the normal arrangement) don't make a penny out of candidates who turn jobs down. Recruitment consultants lose out on their commissions and, to add insult to injury, they stand a chance of getting a flea in their ear from turned-down employers as well.

All these factors are reasons for pointing out to you that you have got a big smoothing exercise on your hands if you turn down a job for which you have been put forward by an agency. Your relationship with the agency doesn't end with this one offer (you hope), so you need to convince them that you're not just a time-waster.

- Make contact with them *before* you make contact with the employer. Let them hear it from you rather than second-hand. In some instances, the recruitment consultant may prefer to take responsibility for informing the employer.

- Explain your reasons for turning the job down. Be as precise as you can. If you've learned anything from your experience that will have a bearing on your targeting benchmarks, tell the recruitment consultant what the lessons are.

- Remember to thank the recruitment consultant for his or her efforts.

- Be prepared for none of this to work. Be prepared to have to go on another agency's books.

5.5 Working your notice

This can be a very difficult period. The longer your notice, the more difficult it will be. Everything we have suggested so far has been geared to keeping things sweet with the employer you are leaving. You should continue to do this by co-operating with any reasonable requests and by not succumbing to the temptation to switch off or adopt a flippant attitude. On the whole, you will probably do best to keep a very low profile.

Offers that are withdrawn

Let's take a look at the case of poor Chris.

> Chris has been head-hunted by a big multinational. His task will be to start up and run a new operation in Northern Ireland. Landing this job was quite an achievement for Chris. Not only will his salary be nearly doubled, but he will also be moving from his present employer (a firm with a turnover of £60m per annum) to one of the major world players, and enhancing his prospects many times over as a result. When he announced he was leaving Chris gave vent to some of his feelings, and as a result he and his boss are scarcely on speaking terms. Chris has now worked out two of his three months' notice.
>
> The bombshell dropped on Monday morning when a letter arrived by recorded delivery just as Chris was leaving for work. It was from his new employers. The gist of the letter was that the group parent company in Vienna had decided to pull out of the Northern Ireland venture. An order had come down to UK Head Office to cancel recruitment plans and withdraw all offers of employment — including Chris's.
>
> Needless to say, Chris was devastated. Already looming in his mind was the thought of having to ask to withdraw his notice and what his boss might say. He might, for instance, say no — in which case, where does that leave Chris?

When you hand in your notice, there is always the temptation to 'say a few things'. All the little niggles you've held in harness over the years can come out. because it doesn't seem to matter any more. Sometimes saying a few things may not be your intention but, if you are asked why you want to leave, the niggles have a habit of surfacing.

Lesson one for handing in your notice is to learn to keep your mouth shut. Don't burn your boats. Don't do anything to queer your relationship with your boss. If you are asked why you want to leave, stick to bland explanations ('An offer I couldn't refuse', etc.) Try not to sound insincere, but say how much you've enjoyed the last few years and how they have contributed greatly to your store of experience.

Is your employer obliged to have you back if you ask to withdraw your notice? The answer is no. But, even if they do, things are never really going to be the same for you, and this is where the damage can lie.

Do you have any legal comeback against a firm that lets you down over a job offer? In terms of breach of contract of employment, the answer again is no. Your contract of employment commences when you start work with a firm, so you can't very well accuse them of breaking something that doesn't yet exist.

They may have acted negligently towards you, but in practice this may be hard to prove. A negligence action is a civil action, and like any civil action must be based on the damages you have sustained: what you have lost in terms of money as a result of the other party's wrongdoing. If you have succeeded in withdrawing your notice and keeping your job with your present employer, then you haven't really lost anything, financially speaking, and putting a value on the damage to your prospects is all a bit vague. In short, think twice before launching into litigation that could be costly (to you).

Companies that are forced to cancel their recruitment plans are perfectly well aware of the problems they are causing. The convention in these situations is to make some offer, or simply to send you a cheque. If they don't, then you may have to make the suggestion. In the final analysis, a letter from your solicitor may do the trick.

The main point here, though, is that if you've had a bad experience like this you've got to be able to put it behind you. Don't let it put you off applying for jobs. The chances of it ever happening again are extremely remote.

Keeping yourself on the market

What many candidates see as a perfectly normal follow-up to getting fixed up is to take themselves off the market by:

- withdrawing from any applications still in the pipeline (including cancelling interviews);
- advising agencies that have been acting for them.

At some stage you will need to do this, but don't do it prematurely. The period up to and just after starting in a new job is one of high risk – a period when you really need to have all your options still open. The time to withdraw from the market is when you feel settled in your new job, and certainly no earlier than when your probationary or trial period expires.

Keeping yourself on the market can be difficult for three reasons.

- You are going to find it harder to generate the same level of application.

- From a purely practical point of view, your availability is impaired because you won't find it easy to get time off for interviews in your first few weeks in a new job.

- You will need to do some explaining if you go to any interviews. Your CV and any application form you have filled in will show your old job as your present job. Your circumstances have changed now, of course. You will have left or you will be on the point of leaving. So what are you doing attending an interview? The best answer you can give is the honest one – you're keeping your options open (just in case). Interviewers will make of this is what they choose, but most of them should see the sense in what you are saying.

5.6 Relocation

We have chosen to deal with this subject separately because it only concerns a small number of people.

Relocation packages

Companies faced with relocating people normally offer to fund some part of the cost. Relocation packages vary enormously. They are normally on offer where:

- the person concerned has been approached;
- the job has been advertised nationally, i.e. candidates are being sought in the knowledge that they will be from all parts of the country and in need of relocating;
- the job has been advertised in an area other than where the

company is based. An example is a company that has moved to a development area (attracted by a grant), then found that the qualified people they need are not available on the local market. They then try to lure such people from other parts of the country. Naturally, they won't stand much chance unless they offer to cover some or all of the costs.

Don't assume a relocation package is available, however, simply because you've got to move from A to B to take the job. When you source jobs that are going to involve relocation, you need to find out whether a package is available and, if so, what it consists of. This information will normally be given to you at an interview. Alternatively, you may need to include it in your questions.

Relocation packages frequently contain a clawback clause. The payments can be repayable (in part or in full) if the relocated employee decides to leave soon after starting. This is something to watch out for if the relocation fails.

Make no bones about it, though, good package or bad package, relocating is going to cost you somewhere along the line, and you need to go into it with your eyes wide open. Just take one example: what if your old property doesn't sell and you're left saddled with the interest on a bridging loan which your new employer is only going to pay for six months? What if you have to drop the price of your property to rock bottom to rid yourself of the millstone round your neck? Thoughts like these can put candidates off the idea of relocating altogether.

The correct approach is to do your sums against a pessimistic scenario (e.g. house not selling). See what the effect on your pocket might be. Compare this with the gains you will be getting from the move (particularly the increased salary).

The point of this exercise is threefold.

- To get your targeting right, and in particular your pay targeting. A relocating job has to be worth it.
- Because of the relocation factor, you may find you are looking for jobs that don't exist (the figure you need isn't available on the market).

- To identify items in the relocation package that might need to be renegotiated before you can consider taking the job (e.g. the period over which the interest on a bridging loan is recoverable).

Taking the risk out of relocating

When you're relocating it's always best, if you can, to do it in stages. Don't burn your boats until:

- you know the job's working out;
- you know the area you're moving to hasn't got hidden snags.

If you've got a family to relocate and properties to buy and sell, it's all the more important not to cut off your line of escape – not until you've made sure you've done the right thing.

Examine, first of all, whether you can commute for a while. Driving for five or six hours a day may not sound very appealing, but it's far better than finding you've made the wrong relocation decision when it's too late. Otherwise, see if you can find rented accommodation locally. Leave the family where they are and travel back home at weekends.

Getting your feet on the ground before embarking on the serious stuff (selling houses, relocating families, having spouses/partners give up their jobs) makes good sense.

5.7 Enticement

Enticing sought-after people from one firm to another has turned into a major industry. Yet succumbing to enticement (accepting the 'offer you can't refuse') is one of the likeliest reasons for you making a bad move.

Money

The traditional way of enticing people from one job to another is to offer them more money. Money has the advantage of being simple and directly quantifiable – and at some point, so the argument goes, we all have a price.

If the job is a big step up the ladder, the difference in salary is a natural consequence. If, however, the move is sideways, the company concerned may have to offer enticement: which means paying more than they did to the previous incumbent (if there was one) or more than they pay to the existing peer group.

Clearly there are dangers from here on. Notably, you will be viewed as 'overpaid', so the prospects for future salary advancement won't be good, and your job performance is going to be under the microscope. The message is: beware if you feel a firm is overstretching itself just to get you on board. The extra cash in your pocket could be short-lived.

Perks

The perks industry really took off in the periods of statutory pay restraint we went through in the 1970s. Firms found they couldn't pay people any more without busting government pay guidelines, so they rewarded them with perks instead. The growth of company-car provision owed much to this period. Bigger and better cars became the name of the game.

Perks have blossomed into an infinite variety of forms: spouses' cars, share options, help with the domestics, help with school fees, subsidised this and subsidised that – the list is almost endless. Perks are frequently used as enticers. The danger here is that you may gloss over the fact that a job falls way short of your targeting benchmarks just because some handsome perk has been included in the package. The kind of car you've always wanted will be particularly hard to say no to.

Job titles

One way to entice people is with job titles. The title 'Director' holds particular allure, and we know of several people who have made conspicuously bad moves for this very reason.

Prospects and promises

Another way in which candidates can be enticed from one company to another is by making promises to them. On the whole, we have coached you to view promises circumspectly and not to attach too much significance to them. There is a distinction, of course, between promises that are attainable in the short term (in defined and realisable circumstances) and those that are some way off in the future and vague. An example of the first is: 'Mr Bloggs is retiring in six months and you will work alongside Mr Bloggs until he goes. When he goes, you will get his job and everything that goes with it.' Given such information, it is reasonable to believe this is precisely what will happen.

Golden hellos

These are up-front, substantial, one-off, lump-sum payments made to newcomers when they join. This enticement device is used almost exclusively in the top-jobs market. The theory behind golden hellos is that they provide companies with an enticement device they can use, without:

- busting existing salary differentials;
- incurring the difficulties involved in enticing candidates with visible perks such as fancy cars that don't figure in the normal range.

It is normal for golden hellos to have a clawback if the newcomer decides to leave (or gets the sack) within a stated period, so do take this into account (don't spend the money straight away, as you may have to give it back).

5.8 Starting a new job

The first few weeks in any new job are usually a bit strange. You won't feel completely at home for several weeks.

Making good early impressions

Good early impressions are important when you start a new job. Good impressions can carry you through the most risky period of your employment – when your new bosses don't know you and when they will judge you by what they see.

When you are starting a new job, you have got a lot of things going in your favour. Notably, the people who selected you will want you to succeed. They will want to feel they've made the right choice and the very last thing they will want to contemplate is you failing, because it will put them back to square one – having to go through the whole time-consuming business of recruiting again.

So where do people go wrong with their early impressions? Often it's not their work which lets them down but aspects of their behaviour.

On your first morning

The classic bad start is not turning up at the correct starting time on your first morning – either arriving late or not turning up at all. Apart from anything else, your non-arrival will mean acute embarrassment for your new boss and you need to be aware of this. Induction arrangements may have to be cancelled or rescheduled, and your new boss may have the job of explaining why you're not there. If he/she doesn't know the reason, then the situation moves from annoyance to exasperation and embarrassment.

What you may not realise, either, is that there is quite a high incidence of people who don't turn up on their first morning. In most cases, it means they've changed their minds. They don't want the job any more and they've not had the decency to let anyone know.

Because of the special problems that surround first mornings, you are well advised to set out for work extra early. Allow for unexpected bottlenecks or trains arriving late. In any event, the journey is new to you, and the chances are this will be first occasion you've attempted it at peak times. If you should find yourself running late, get ready to make a phone call and get ready to make it well before the time you're due to start. Don't have your boss glancing up at the clock and wondering where you are.

Even with this level of communication, a late start on your first morning won't be viewed kindly. You've still got an uphill struggle on your hands to get your credibility back. Any more lates and you really are inviting trouble.

Of course the ultimate stroke of bad luck is to be sick on day one. This is really a case of crawling in if you can, or getting on that phone again well before starting time if you can't.

Another reason for failing to start on the first morning is arriving back late from holidays. Some candidates choose to go off on holiday immediately before starting a new job. Their reasons vary.

- It's a convenient way of working out notice, especially if they've got some holiday entitlement left which they need to take (they would lose it otherwise).

- They feel it's a way of recharging their batteries.

- They may have been unable to have their holidays earlier because of job-hunting activities.

- If they've been unemployed, it's an opportunity to have a last fling with what's left of their redundancy money.

Ringing in with your excuses is quite hard if you happen to be sitting it out in a Spanish airport, facing a five-hour delay to your homebound flight. By all means have a holiday before starting a new job, but make sure you are going to get back with plenty of time to spare.

On your first morning it's important, too, that you take with you everything you've been asked to take. Failing to have your bank details or your birth certificate or anything else you've been asked to bring along won't do you a lot of good on the early-impressions front.

Finally, on the first morning dress up, not down. Remember that on your first morning you will be meeting people, so you will want to look your best.

Over the first few weeks

You can cement your good early impressions by continuing to watch your Ps and Qs over the next few weeks. Again, being late or having time off are flashpoints, and you should do all that you can to ensure that your time-keeping and attendance are flawless.

If you are ill, then you need to do two things:

- follow the company's procedures for notifying absence diligently (phoning in, sending in medical certificates when they become due, etc.);
- keep up the communication with your boss.

Here is a final tip: when you start in a new job, try to resist telling people how you did things in the last firm – unless you are asked, that is. It can be annoying.

> **LESSON 6** Using your experience
>
> The object of this final lesson is to make you appreciate the value of completing and learning from your experience (good or bad). The corollary to this appreciation is that you don't go on making the same mistakes over and over again.
>
> On the subject of targeting, you will remember that we encouraged you to view targets as flexible and dynamic. They should be subject to change, and the changes should be made in the light of your experience.
>
> The job market isn't some homogeneous entity which behaves in exactly the same way throughout. It consists of hundreds of thousands of tiny little niches.
>
> You will learn about your niche of the market from one source only and that is by being active in it. You will learn, for example, what the market pays – if there is a going rate (a narrow band) or if there is a wide range of pay on offer. You will learn if there are many firms in the market for your type of skills or if you only have limited sources of employment. From making applications and from attending interviews you will build up a store of extremely useful and up-to-date information. This will tell you:
>
> - if you are targeting too high, to the point where you are targeting jobs that don't exist;
> - if there are other elements in your targeting that mean you're looking for a job that doesn't exist;
> - if you're under-targeting, i.e. selling yourself cheap – a problem normally associated with people who work for firms that pay poorly.

The point to emphasise here is the importance of completing, not giving up until you have accumulated sufficient experience to enable you to form an overview of:

- what the market has to offer;
- how it views you.

One of the difficulties for people who are successful first time with job applications is that they don't learn a lot about their niche market. They are in and out of it too fleetingly. They don't learn, for instance, if they are under-targeting. Without knowing it, they may have moved from a very poorly paid job into one that is still slightly below the market rate. If they had been on the market a bit longer, they would have seen that there were some much better jobs on offer.

Experience helps in other ways, too, apart from targeting.

- You get better at sourcing, notably proactive sourcing such as cold calling.
- You get better at keeping control of your applications.
- You get better at handling interviews – certainly at spotting the questions they don't ask.
- You get better at dealing with the turn-downs.
- You develop much sharper instincts. You get good at spotting rogue employers.

It is quite surprising what candidates can learn from being active in their own niche of the job market. They become founts of information on the subject.

The point of this lesson is to try to get you to move away from viewing your job applications in terms of successes and failures. View them as experiences instead.

Summary

After going through the process of applying for a job and attending the interviews, getting the offer in your hand should be a moment of elation. Your approach has worked and you have seen off any competition. But now comes the difficult bit – deciding whether to go for what's been put in front of you or whether to leave it alone; whether to stick to old familiar territory or whether to set off on the long lonely walk into the unknown.

Changing jobs is far more risky these days, and this is a fact we have to learn to live with. Recovering from bad moves isn't easy, either. It could be several years before you get your career back on track, so it is all the more important that you view your job offers dispassionately. Forget the 'feel-good factor' and the flattery. Take a long, hard look at what's on the table before you say yes.

The 'offer you can't refuse'

In this chapter we have looked at the methods of enticement firms use. Succumbing to enticement is the biggest single reason for people making bad moves. Dazzled by the cash or the job title or the fancy car, they ignore the obvious warning signs flashing at them. 'I knew I was making a mistake . . . ' you hear them say afterwards, but then of course it's too late. Need we point out that the extra £10,000 a year won't do you much good if the job only lasts six months?

These days, all job offers should be seen as refusable.

Keeping your options open

Having assembled all the relevant information on a job, and without being too inflexible, the first point to establish is whether it meets your targeting benchmarks. By taking the job will you be achieving what you set out to achieve? Thinking about this will expose two potential dangers.

- Are you allowing disenchantment with your present job to colour your view of what's being offered to you? In other words, because you're feeling fed up you may be seeing the job in a better light than it deserves.

- Are you allowing yourself to be swayed by persuasion (employers who sell you jobs)?

Having gone through our various pre-acceptance stops and checks, and given that the signals are all positive, there is still no absolute guarantee your move is going to be the right one. The truth of the matter is you won't know this until you've been doing the job for a while, and there is still always the eventuality of you finding you've made a mistake.

Given the uncertainty of new jobs in new firms, given the multitude of things that can go wrong, we have counselled you to try to keep your options open as far as you can. In particular:

- leave your old firm on the best terms possible – keep the door open for U-turns;.

- keep yourself active on the job market – carry on with any applications you've still got in the pipeline;

- if relocation is required, relocate in stages – so you won't be selling your house and uprooting your family before the job's proved itself to you.

Questions and answers

Offers of employment – snags in the small print

Q *I have recently received an offer of employment from a company (a good job), but when I read through their terms and conditions of employment I came across a clause which was not to my liking. It stipulated that I had to be prepared to relocate to any part of the UK as and when directed.*

I rang the company straight away and pointed out to them that there had been no mention of this requirement at any of the interviews. I explained that because of my personal circumstances (husband with good job locally; children approaching GCSE examinations, etc.) I could not contemplate moving home.

Their attitude was quite laid back. They said the clause was a standard item and 'not to worry about it' because it only applied to people in operational grades. My worries persisted, though, and I ended up turning the job down. Did I do right?

A Presumably, the worry that persisted was that the relocation clause might be invoked at some future date and by then the reassurances you received might be conveniently forgotten. This is, of course, one of the problems of dealing with people you don't really know.

An alternative approach to yours would have been to ask the company to put it in writing to you that the clause only applied to operational grades. If they were telling you the truth then they should have had no problem with this.

Variations on what was said at the interview

Q *I received an offer of employment from a local company which employs around 150 people. The salary quoted was £18,500 p.a., yet in the advertisement for the job a figure of £20,000 was mentioned. The job is a good job (much better than the one I've got) and I wouldn't want to jeopardise my position by appearing to be quibbling about the salary. What do you suggest I do?*

A Go back to your targeting benchmarks. Does £18,500 match up to your original pay expectations? If it does – and providing everything else is matched and your instincts aren't screaming warnings at you – take the job.

Offers of employment: a better job in the pipeline

Q *I was shortlisted for two jobs, A and B. Job B is better than Job A, both in terms of salary and long-term prospects. I have been offered Job A and the company concerned is pressing me for an answer. I have phoned the Job B company to explain my predicament, but it seems they won't be able to let me have a decision for at least a fortnight. I honestly don't feel I can keep Job A open for as long as that. What do I do?*

A Take Job A. If Job B comes through, take that in preference. Tell the Job A company you have changed your mind because you have had another offer. The job market is not a tidy place, so you will rarely, if ever, be in a situation where all the jobs you have applied for are lined up in an orderly fashion for you to choose from.

Losing the right to a long period of notice

Q *I have been offered a top management job with a leading plc. The job is subject to six months' notice on either side, which bothers me because I currently enjoy a three-year rolling contract. Six months' notice is standard terms with the plc so they won't negotiate. Is this a case of 'take it or leave it' – or is there anything I haven't considered?*

A In public companies two- and three-year rolling contracts have come in for a bit of flak in recent years – notably from institutional shareholders. The trend now is for foreshortened periods of notice for senior job-holders.

The risky part of any new job is at the beginning, so one way the plc could address your concerns is with an arrangement like this:

- employment is guaranteed for the first two or three years (the risk period) by means of a fixed-term contract;
- when the guaranteed period expires the contract transfers onto the normal six months' notice basis.

What you need to watch out for with these arrangements is that the transition between fixed-term and rolling notice is covered so that employment can't be brought abruptly to a close when the fixed period expires. This can best be achieved by having the two arrangements running concurrently; so, in the beginning, the notice required to terminate the contract is whichever happens to be the longest – either the unexpired portion of the fixed term or the six months.

SIX

JOINING THE COMPLEMENTARY WORKFORCE

Today there is a bewildering assortment of short-term, temporary and assignment-based jobs, and firms use an increasing number of self-employed people to provide outsourced or in-house services. In this chapter we will look at the so-called complementary sector (the flexible workforce) and examine how complementary-sector employment can be incorporated into your career options.

6.1 Temping

This is the sort of complementary-sector employment we are most familiar with. There is a demand for temps in practically every walk of life. Firms who use temps usually do so for one of two reasons:

- to fill a gap in the ranks when (someone is off sick, on holiday, on maternity leave, etc.);
- to fill a short-term need, such as an upsurge in work that isn't forecast to last.

Temps can be:

- employed by a firm (direct);
- employed by an agency;
- self-employed people.

A period of temporary employment is either fixed (i.e. the finishing date will be pre-determined) or open-ended.

Temping for an agency

To a large extent, the market for temporary staff has been cornered by agencies. If you're looking for temporary work, therefore, the easiest way to access it is by registering with the right agency.

We covered choosing the right agency when we looked at agencies as sources of permanent employment (see page 80). The rules for choosing agencies for temporary work are much the same. Mainly, you must make sure the agency covers the occupational group to which you belong.

Measure an agency by:

- its ability to provide you with work as and when you want it (in turn this is a measure of the agency's client base).
- what it is prepared to pay you;
- its commitment to you (more important if you are viewing temping on a long-term rather than a stopgap basis). Examples of commitment are provision of holiday pay, sick pay and, in some cases, training.

In turn, an agency will expect from you:

- availability: that you can be contacted quickly and easily (telephone contactability again!) and that you will be available to do assignments as and when they ask;
- competence: that you will be able to carry out the assignment to the satisfaction of their client.

Applying to an agency to be a temp is a bit like applying for any other kind of job. Agencies advertise for temps (usually in the 'Situations Vacant' columns), or you can just ring them up. Interviews with agencies vary from highly professional affairs (with tests) to the barely perfunctory.

Because at the start you don't know how any of these agencies are going to perform, pick out three with a view to whittling them down. Doing an assignment for one agency, though, means you're not available for the others. This can and does lead to conflict and the agency you're saying sorry to may quietly drop you (the whittling-down is done for you).

When you're temping, you can choose your hours of work, though naturally there is more call for people who can work 'normal' hours. For example, if your temping revolves around some normal office-type occupation there won't be much call for you if you're only available at night.

The advantages of temping via an agency are:

- they find the work for you;
- the better ones able to provide you with a steady flow of work;
- you will have one employer – the agency.

The main drawback is the level of pay.

Temping direct

Sometimes firms advertise temporary vacancies. Sometimes people get offered temporary work as a result of their proactive sourcing. The pros and cons of temping for a firm direct are roughly the reverse of the pros and cons of temping via an agency. The disadvantages are:

- you have to find the work;
- it will be hard to sustain an even flow of work;
- each assignment will be with a new employer.

Temping direct is usually better paid, however.

Temping as an option

In modern careers, temping can be useful:

- where a permanent job is only available on a part-time basis – the shortfall in earnings can be made up by temping;
- where you're starting up as a freelancer and you need another little earner while you're building up business;

- where you're established as a freelancer but you hit a bad patch (e.g. lose an important contract) – temping will help you through;
- where you're trying to start a career: you can do the job but need to be able to show you've had some experience – temping can provide you with experience.

> Jeremy was made redundant from a top management job two months ago. He is 40 and deeply concerned that his career has now suffered a major setback.
>
> As a result of mailing a few firms, Jeremy gets an interview with Mr Plummer, the Chief Executive of a company he used to view as an indirect competitor. The interview follows a strange pattern, but at the end of it Mr Plummer offers him a temporary job, a six-month assignment nurturing a new product onto the market. After six months, Mr Plummer explains, the new product will integrate into the company's existing range – and the need for nurturing will disappear. There is no permanent job at the end, Mr Plummer emphasises.
>
> Jeremy thanks Mr Plummer and asks for 48 hours to think things over. Mr Plummer agrees to this.
>
> Back home, Jeremy discusses Mr Plummer's offer with his wife and, over the phone, with his brother, who is the Human Resources Director of a large plc. All three are of the same mind: that Jeremy should turn Mr Plummer's offer down. Their reasons are as follows.
>
> ❏ The salary mentioned works out at around £30,000 p.a. Jeremy earned £40,000 in the last job. The view, therefore, is that he will be selling himself short.
>
> ❏ It will take Jeremy away from his real task, which is getting his career back on track. Most notably, however, he will be sacrificing his availability.
>
> ❏ The probability is that Mr Plummer is only looking to pick Jeremy's brains.

Jeremy may be lucky in his search for another top management job and we wish him well. With luck, he won't be out of work

much longer. What, however, he, his wife and his brother have missed is the opportunity for visibility that Mr Plummer's offer presents.

With some justification, temping has been described as a way of getting into organisations through the back door. The fact that you're there and known to everyone puts you in definite pole position if any good jobs should come up. You may even turn out to be in a one-horse race. In short, it's a great way of accessing the invisible market. The visibility doesn't just work for you during the period of your employment, either. Your face will be remembered for some time.

We can recall many cases of unemployed people who have accessed good jobs by using temping as a stepping-stone. So, if you're unemployed and find yourself with an offer of temporary work, don't (like Jeremy) worry about:

- having your brains picked – in fact, the more opportunity you've got to show off your skills and experience the better;
- being paid less (within reason) – what matters is the job and the salary that your visibility could access for you.

Admittedly, loss of availability is a problem with taking temporary assignments, but this can be counteracted by reaching agreement with your employer, in advance, that you can:

- take phone calls at work;
- have (unpaid) time off for interviews.

Wanting to get back into a mainstream career job is a perfectly respectable aim and most employers of temps will be entirely sympathetic and happy to help.

6.2 Contracts

The distinction between temping and contracts is blurred. Some people, for instance, would refer to the kind of arrangement Mr Plummer was suggesting to Jeremy as a medium-term contract.

Contractual terms

Like temporary employment, contracts have an envisaged end. This time, the end is more likely to be determined by:

- a fixed calendar date;
- completion of a project.

Depending on their length, contracts are described as short-, medium- or long-term. The last would tend to run into years. With some contracts, there is provision for termination by notice. Otherwise, the ramifications are as follows.

- If you want to get out of a contract, you need to do it by negotiation and agreement.
- If the contract-provider wants to get out of a contract, they have to pay you off for the unexpired portion.

Sources of contracts

Firms (end-users) engage people on contracts and you will see them advertising in the press. A lot of overseas postings are on one- or two-year contracts. You can source contracts from end-users either by scanning the ads (trade journals can be useful) or you can engage proactive sourcing methods, targeting firms you have seen advertising contracts in the past. With proactive sourcing, make it clear that you are looking for contracts rather than permanent employment.

There are firms who specialise in contracts (for example, contract design offices) and you can pick these out of local trade directories (you may know some already). Generally speaking, any businesses describing themselves as consultants or providers of management services are good sources of contracts. A quick phone call will tell you whether you are barking up the right tree or not.

Some professional institutions act as a clearing-house for contracts. If you're in a professional institution, check your membership literature or give them a quick call.

Viewing contracts as an option

Why do people do contract work? The usual answer is the money. Contracts pay well, normally much more than what you would expect to earn in a permanent job. Some people make a career out of working contracts. The drawbacks are as follows.

- Contracts tend to dry up when times get hard. In a recession it is usually the contract sector that gets hit first.
- Moving from contracts back into normal mainstream employment can be difficult. It is not uncommon to find employers hostile to ex-contract people ('Only interested in the money', 'Will be back on contracts the minute things pick up').
- Prospects for promotion are usually nil.
- Some providers of contract services expect you to work anywhere and everywhere. You can find yourself living out of a suitcase, which may not be to your liking.

Apart from the money, there are other advantages of contract working for people in careers.

- If you want to work abroad, a good way of dipping your toe in the water is to get an overseas contract with a UK firm.
- Sometimes careers have natural hiatuses – times when you don't feel like throwing yourself back into the thick of things, at least not straight away. Doing a contract job is one way of inserting a semicolon in your career. The fact that it has a defined beginning and a defined end means that the emotional involvement (the psychological bonding) is minimal.
- Consultants, etc. are usually clued up to all the latest techniques, so the experience you get and the skills you learn from working on contracts can be very marketable.

6.3 Self-employment (freelancing)

In some commercial sectors working freelance is quite commonplace, whereas in others it is still novel or unknown.

Outsourcing

One of the interesting trends of recent years has been larger firms outsourcing their specialist work and concentrating on what they see as their core functions, e.g. sales, manufacturing, distribution. An example is the firm which closes its in-house pensions department and outsources the work to a firm of professional pensions' advisors.

In one of the questions at the end of Chapter 1, there was a Human Resources Manager about to be made redundant because the Human Resources Department in his firm was closing down. Part of our advice to him was to find out what was happening to the HR work. Was it, for example, going to be outsourced? If so, two options might present themselves.

- Putting himself (and his colleagues) forward as potential suppliers of the outsourced service.

- Getting a job with the firm the outsourced work will be going to.

Of course, as so often happens in these situations, there may be no intention to outsource. The plan, if there is one, may be simply to dump the HR responsibilities onto line managers, and muddle along from there. If this is the case, our HR Manager may have to implant the idea of outsourcing into the minds of his top management. Why should they go for it? Surprisingly enough, the idea of an incumbent with all the knowledge locked in his head wanting to provide the service from outside may be instantly appealing (something they've never thought of).

On page 89, we left Ian, our Health and Safety Advisor, flogging away at his proactive sourcing. Ian is in a one-off specialist role in an employers' association, and he has no upward career route available to him. So what about Ian going along to his directors and putting forward the idea of outsourcing the H and S work to him? Ian would get to broaden his career horizons. It could even be the beginning of Ian and Associates (Health and Safety Consultants).

Why should the directors buy it? First, if they've got a high opinion of Ian they won't want to lose his services and, second, if they've got any sense, they'll see that an ambitious 38-year-old will not be satisfied with doing the same job till the day he retires.

One of the critical points when going self-employed is the start-up, and it will help you enormously if you can take all or part of your old job with you. This is the opportunity that outsourcing offers.

Self-employed options

There are a number of different ways in which you can operate as a self-employed person:

- as a temp;
- on a contract;
- as an outsourced service provider;
- working in-house;
- doing combinations of any of these; even combining them with a mix of part-time PAYE jobs (portfolio working).

Going freelance

As a self-employed person, you will be responsible for:

- marketing yourself;
- making sure you do the job properly and meeting your deadlines;
- keeping the records you need to keep;
- paying your suppliers and making sure your clients pay you;
- managing your cashflow – making sure you've always got enough money in the bank;
- deciding what to pay yourself.

This list is not exhaustive, but is meant to illustrate how, if you're moving into self-employment from a normal PAYE job, you will find yourself shouldering responsibilities that you have never had before.

Making mistakes

If you are going into self-employment for the first time, accept that you are going to make mistakes. Everyone does. The important thing is to learn from your mistakes and not to go on making them. The main pitfalls for the newly self-employed are:

- overspending (make a note to put the new sports car on next year's shopping list);
- not paying enough attention to administration;
- failing to pay tax, NI contributions and VAT on time, and as a result getting into trouble with the authorities;
- giving up too soon.

All these early pitfalls are avoidable.

Selling yourself

Unless you are particularly well endowed with contacts, your first problem is going to be getting enough work. Don't bank on promises people have made to you. Don't bank on big mailshots, either. The reality of setting up on your own is that success takes time. Here are a few tips for starting up as a freelancer.

- At the beginning, your best potential source of work is where you're known best, i.e. your old firm. This means: leaving on good terms; and plugging the outsourcing option for all it's worth. Don't assume, though, that your old firm will go on supplying you with work. Faces change, as do attitudes; but a good, steady income during your start-up period will be an enormous help to you (your bouncing board).

- Tap into your networks and contacts: again, take the view that you will have most chance of getting work where your face is known. Be prepared to bend a bit here, too. For example, if you've set yourself up as a freelance Word-processing Trainer and one of your contacts comes along and asks you to word-process a batch of letters (i.e. secretarial work), don't view this as something beneath you or as something you don't do. Use your skills-base flexibly. All that matters at this point is having some money coming in.

- Keep all your options in the frame. This includes doing part-time jobs or temping part-time – in fact, anything to keep the wolf from the door. Be prepared to 'mix 'n' match'.

- Keep on top of administration (never easy when you're busy); make it part of your daily and weekly routines.

- Find someone to talk to (your nearest and dearest may be the best candidate). Facing the black moments can be lonely otherwise.

Is freelancing for you?

Hitherto a lot of the discussion about going freelance has centred around:

- whether you're the right type;
- whether it's something you've really (seriously) thought through.

A common view is that it's a strange and risky thing to want to do – or it's only for those with entrepreneurial leanings. Our opinion is different. In the future, we see freelancing forming part of more and more people's careers – an option you can't and shouldn't overlook.

What does freelancing offer?

- First, the experience. You get to learn about the way business works. You will broaden your experience outside your own immediate field. Your experience is no longer 'one company' either. You get to see how other firms work.

- If you play your cards right and you work hard, you can make a lot of money, in most cases more than you will ever make in PAYE jobs.

- Because you will, in all likelihood, have more than one client, your livelihood will no longer depend on the fortunes of one firm.

- Like temps, freelancers are very visible – the kind of people who get offered jobs because they're there.

- You will be moving in the big wide world. Your professional networks will extend as a result of this.

- It can lead to great things. Many highly successful businesses began with someone, somewhere, deciding to go freelance.
- It can be a good option for people who see themselves in the 'too old' category. If you're freelancing no one will care whether you're 35 or 55. All you'll be judged on is whether you can do the job or not.

When to call it a day

The way to avoid some of the bigger risks in working freelance is to know when to stop. Not making enough money is a clear enough reason to quit and, even if you fudge the decision at first, sooner or later the lack of funds will prompt you to act. Here it helps to view your excursion into freelancing not in terms of failure but as an episode in your career: something you actually did, something you gained experience from – and something you stopped doing when it became prudent. All that matters is you took the right decision when it became necessary. You kept control.

Sometimes, however, the signals to call it a day are less easy to read.

> Amelia is a Software Trainer. She has been working freelance for five years, previous to which she worked for a leading software house. Amelia went freelance because she saw the opportunity to make more money. In this she was right. As a freelancer she can earn £8–10,000 more than the software house paid her. The problem for Amelia is that she's not sure where her career is going. The money she's making is good, but ideally she would like to get out of the training role into a management job. She is 42 now and beginning to think she's missed the boat.

Career advancement (moving on and moving up) has difficulties for the self-employed. Two stumbling blocks present themselves.

- Going solo means no longer being part of some structure, hence no longer having internal promotion routes available to you.

- The success freelancers have is all their own. It goes with them personally, and this is what can make it hard for them to escape from being hands-on. For example, if Amelia tried to resolve her career problem by growing her one-woman business into a software training company she could find herself coming under pressure from clients to continue to provide the training herself. Anyone else (e.g. a trainer she recruits to work for her) will be seen as second best.

The bottom line is that self-employed people can start to under-achieve but, because the money still looks good, the fact that they're under-achieving is camouflaged. For many self-employed people, realisation only comes when they see former colleagues (people who didn't go freelance) doing better than they are.

You may be working freelance because you've got designs on starting your own business or because you don't want to do anything else. Otherwise, be quite clear about where you see your exit point. View it a bit like a job with no prospects. Once you've made the money, had the experience, proved whatever it was you wanted to prove to yourself – leave it there. Go back to reviewing your options. Work out your next step.

• WARNING •

Leaving freelancing to go back into mainstream career employment can sometimes mean 'moving sideways to move upwards'. For example, Amelia could find it difficult going out on the market in search of, say, a Data Processing Manager's job (she has no management experience). What she may have to consider instead is targeting trainers' jobs in organisations where the promotion prospects are good and accepting that this may mean a drop in earnings.

The warning is this. Don't let big earnings trap you into freelancing to the point where you're under-achieving. Take on board all we said about the ups and downs of earnings in modern careers. Plan your finances accordingly.

Once you've decided to call it a day, make a mental note that freelancing is something you may want to go back to. The experience you had first time round will then stand you in good stead.

Summary

Career power is the art of the possible – using what's there and turning it to your advantage. Three things about the complementary sector are important:

- it's there (accessible);
- it's big;
- it's getting bigger.

So don't ignore the complementary sector. It contributes to the richness and diversity of modern careers. It could enter into your options if you are in one of the following situations.

- You are trying to start a career: you are looking for ways in and getting experience (see Chapter 7).
- You are out of work: you can afford to take risks and the visibility provided by temping or freelancing can give you a stepping-stone back into a permanent job.
- You are viewing yourself as 'too old': your best assets are your experience and your ability to do the job.
- You are contemplating a career change but you want to dip your toe in the water first (take a fortnight's holiday and temp in whatever your chosen activity happens to be).
- You want to make more money – working freelance or on a contract can provide the opportunity.
- You want to work freelance for the experience or to prove something to yourself.

Within this framework, there are lots of opportunities to 'mix 'n' match' too. For example:

- temping for an agency part-time while starting up on your own;

- combining part-time permanent jobs with temping part time and/or working freelance; really doing whatever suits (either short-term or long-term).

View the complementary sector for what it is – something that is always there; something you can move into and move out of when it suits your purposes. The main danger with complementary-sector working is letting it swallow you up, e.g. temping or working freelance for too long and under-achieving as a result.

Finally, if you're using temping or freelancing as a way of making yourself visible so you can source permanent core-sector jobs, remember:

- to give it your best shot;
- to make sure you're visible in the right quarters (the person with the power to say yes needs to know you're there);
- to make it known you're after a permanent job;
- if you finish the assignment, to leave a copy of your CV;
- to put the firm on your cold-calling list.

Questions and answers

Tax and portfolio working

Q Will I have any problems tax-wise by combining freelance work with my part-time PAYE job?

A None, providing you declare everything. If in doubt, consult an accountant.

Self-employed with just one client – could I be assessed for PAYE?

Q I very recently became self-employed, but up to now all the work I have done has been for one firm. A friend warned me that in this situation the Inland Revenue can choose to view me as an employee, meaning my client can have a PAYE demand slapped on them. Is this true? Naturally I don't want my one-and-only client to start viewing me as a problem.

A The Inland Revenue has guidelines on how they determine whether someone is genuinely self-employed or not. These guidelines largely revolve around the extent to which you are a free agent. For instance, if you only do work for one client, if this client supplies you with the equipment and materials to do the job, if they control how and when you work, if they pay your expenses – these are all factors which can contribute to you being viewed as employed. How do these situations get picked up? If your client has a tax audit there's a fair chance they will get asked questions about any self-employed people they use.

Our advice is to:

- get some more clients on your books;
- make sure you're raising sales invoices for your work as opposed to receiving payments on a regular (e.g. monthly) basis;
- register for VAT (unless there are over-riding reasons why you shouldn't);
- provide your own equipment/stationery;
- use and pay for your own car;
- meet your own costs (expenses). By all means take them into account when you establish your prices, but don't bill them separately or, worse still, hand your client a petty cash voucher or expenses claim form.

Self-employed – is there a stigma?

Q *I am told the job market is hostile to people who are, or have been, self-employed. Is this true?*

A Remember the hidden criteria? All employers are different. They all have their own little preferences and prejudices. So, yes, there will be some who see people who've worked freelance as rebellious go-it-aloners, or money freaks, or both. Equally, there will be some who see the freelance experience as evidence of grit, determination and someone's ability to stand on their own two feet. As freelancing, particularly short-term freelancing, becomes more and more commonplace, there is less tendency to view it as being any of these things. The same goes for temping and working on contracts. Here it helps to bear in mind that interviewers and decision-makers are people in careers too. There is a greater chance these days that they will also have spent some time in the complementary sector.

SEVEN

STARTING A CAREER

For many younger people, the problem has been getting started in a career – finding someone who is prepared to give them training and experience.

7.1 The market for first jobs in careers

In recent years there has been an increase in the number of young people going into higher education. This means that there is more demand for career starting points. On the supply side, however, two things have happened:

- there has been a decline in the number of training providers – big firms have gone or they don't take trainees any more, either because they don't have the resources or because they no longer think it's their job to provide people with training;
- there are more small firms; these, generally speaking, don't have the time or the resources to provide training, and tend to want people with experience.

The picture, therefore, is one of more and more people chasing fewer and fewer jobs.

Career power, to remind you, is the art of the possible – using what's there and turning it to your advantage. Now let's apply this to getting you started off in your career.

Acquiring some basic skills

A lot of what we do at work comes down to basic skills. If anything, basic skills are becoming increasingly important for the following reasons.

- The cost-cutting and trimming-down execises of recent years have taken away a lot of administrative and support staff. Hence people in business aren't surrounded by armies of secretaries, assistants and office juniors any more. If there's routine work to be done, they do it themselves.

- More firms are small ones, and many big firms have been broken down into small, autonomous cells. Life in small units has always centred around the basics.

If you are looking to start a career, you can make yourself more marketable by acquiring some basic skills. Examples of basic skills are the ability to:

- drive;
- word-process a simple letter using modern PC software;
- carry out a basic conversation in at least two widely used modern languages;
- give first aid.

The interesting thing about these basic skills is that they are easy to acquire. In most cases, your local evening institute will provide the courses. For a small investment they will add greatly to your saleability – particularly to the small, busy firms that make up much of the modern market. Someone who can hop in a car and run an errand, send out an urgent letter, speak to the German customers in their own language and help meet the Health and Safety at Work Act's requirements for trained first-aid personnel will be viewed as a very useful person indeed.

The 'Trojan horse' technique

For all the reasons we've given in the book, the world of careers isn't a tidy place any more. There are still big firms with intakes of graduates every year, but you can no longer rely on these. The chances are, increasingly, that you will have to find other, less straightforward ways of getting into a career. In short, having a degree or the equivalent of an degree guarantees you nothing.

On the positive side, though, there are lots of opportunities for worming your way into organisations and attacking them from inside (the 'Trojan horse' technique). Let's take firm Z as a typical modern employer. Firm Z doesn't take on graduate trainees, but they do need people in routine jobs, many of whom will be taken on as temps. The trick is to get yourself in, doing a routine job. The art of the possible comes into play again – the routine jobs are there, but the career starts aren't.

Revisiting your CV

The first thing to do with your newly acquired basic skills is to put them on your CV. Think about your CV, too. Is it right for the 'Trojan horse' technique? For instance, if in your little personal profile you are describing yourself as 'an ambitious 22-year-old graduate, keen to start a career in industrial management', is this going to strike any chords with a harassed employer looking for a Telephone Sales Clerk? The likely outcome of this bit of self-interrogation is that you decide you need two CVs, and possibly more.

At this point, it will help to reflect on what employers have against using graduates and graduate equivalents in jobs that don't call for anything special in the way of qualifications. What are their big fears?

- First, the cost. Won't well-qualified people be looking for a lot of money?
- Won't they be looking for advancement, too? Many employers these days (not just small firms) feel they can't offer advancement.
- Won't they find the work boring? Won't they soon get fed up and leave – meaning that the employer is back with the unwelcome job to having to recruit again?

Bearing in mind that the job of your CV is to get you interviews, these are the kind of fears you've got to overcome to avoid being put on the 'Not selected for interview' pile. In this situation, one of the worst things you can do is make a big issue out of the fact that you are playing downmarket. Let the reader of your CV see that you are doing something you at least consider normal.

Let's now see what your second CV needs to be saying. Here we need to go into a bit more detail about the type of 'Trojan horse' job you are targeting, so let's assume you're a business graduate with career ambitions in sales and marketing. A suitable 'Trojan horse' job for you might be in telesales (sometimes referred to as internal sales), where employers will be looking for bright young people who come across well on the phone. Some numeracy skills may also be useful.

So, to get interviews for these kind of jobs, what messages do you need to be articulating via your CV? The factual part – your personal information, your education and qualifications, what you do in your spare time – clearly remains the same. Any tinkering you will be doing will tend to be in three areas.

- Your personal profile. Here you can describe yourself as a well-educated, keen-to-get-into-sales type: good on the phone, with a good head for figures, and looking for your first job in telesales. In other words, you're telling the firm that the job they've got is precisely the kind of job you're looking for. Make the match for them.

- The detail of what you did at university. Is there anything (e.g. a project) which has any bearing on telesales? If so, bring it to the fore (a strong point).

- Employment experience. Like most students, you've probably done an assortment of vacation jobs. Bear in mind that many of the dealing-with-people skills involved in waiting on tables or working behind bars or in shops transfer neatly into telesales. Again, bring these to the fore. Say you enjoyed these jobs.

7.2 Sourcing

Remember that you are trying to source two very different kinds of job: career starts (e.g. graduate traineeships) and routine jobs you can work the 'Trojan horse' technique with. Don't, however, send conflicting messages to employers, i.e. don't try to source career starts and 'Trojan horse' jobs with the same firm. Avoid the kind of letter that reads: 'Dear Sir, I am a 22-year-old business studies graduate seeking to start a career in sales and marketing and wondering if you have any suitable positions. Alternatively, I would be quite happy to consider jobs in internal sales . . . '. You are making it abundantly clear to the employer that you view the internal sales jobs as second best, which won't endear you to anyone.

Newspapers

Whereas graduate intakes may be thin on the ground, in the local papers there is certainly no shortage of ads for potential 'Trojan horse' jobs, confirming that the difficulty here isn't sourcing but knowing which ones to apply for and which ones to leave alone (more on this in section 7.4).

Agencies

Agencies are always worth registering with (selectively) because they can help you access the invisible market. When registering with general agencies, remember that temporary jobs can make good 'Trojan horses' too. In other words make it clear to the agencies that you are interested in either temporary or permanent positions.

• WARNING •

For many well-qualified people the big issue with 'Trojan horse' jobs is the money. Something you need to get clear in your head at the outset is that you can't dictate terms to the market. If you approach 'Trojan horse' jobs with graduate-level expectations regarding pay, you won't get anywhere. Accept that you may be looking at a half, or even a third, of what the graduate market has taught you to expect. Console yourself with the fact that you won't be on low salaries for long (if you are, you're doing something wrong). With money, the time to start calling the tune is when you've got some experience to bargain with.

Professional networking

This is where we start to enter the world of proactive sourcing, where the idea is to attack the invisible market where there is less competition about.

Vacation jobs and work-based parts of college courses (e.g. industrial placements) bring you into contact with people who, though they may not be influential themselves, may be able to carry out some soundings for you. If your contact happens to be someone for whom you've done work, and who will put in a good word for you, then so much the better. The spin-offs from having done vacation work in firms that can supply the kind of jobs you are targeting are immense. Some seed-sowing while you are still there ('I'll be looking for a job next year') does no harm.

Another way of developing networks is to make sure you join your appropriate professional institution (at whatever grade of membership you qualify for, e.g. student, graduate). Apart from being the right thing to do anyway (for future career advancement reasons), joining a professional institution can bring you into contact with precisely the right kind of people. Most of these institutions have a network of local branches, which meet from time to time and organise activities. Secretaries and/or Membership Secretaries of these local branches can be very helpful to newly qualified people.

Remember, however, only to use professional networking to source career jobs (not 'Trojan horses').

Advertising yourself

This may be worth a try, again as a way of sourcing career jobs on the invisible market. When we discussed how to advertise yourself (see page 86), we gave a special mention to professional journals. A lot of professional journals are published by professional institutions, of course, and this is another good reason for making sure you join.

Cold calling and mail/faxshots

These are the most commonly used proactive sourcing methods. You can use them for any kind of target (career jobs and 'Trojan horses'), and the way to proceed is as described in Chapter 3. In selecting firms for this kind of approach, you should bear two points in mind.

- As advised earlier, avoid sourcing career jobs and 'Trojan horses' from the same firm at the same time. This sends out confused messages.

- Don't write off firms that have already taken on their complement of graduates. Frequently there is fall-out from big intakes (people who quit, people who don't make the grade) and the firms concerned are left scratching round for replacements. If the fall-out occurs early on, the replacements might come from a reserve list (the near misses) but, if some time has passed, the reserves may well have found themselves other jobs. Here is where a phone call or a letter out of the blue can hit the target at precisely the right time. Remember that firms won't be falling over themselves to go through the rigmarole of interviews, assessment centres, psychometric tests, etc., just to fill one vacancy. What we are saying here is there's a chance that the selection procedures won't be quite so stringent.

Structuring your sourcing

Ideally, of course, you want to step right into a career job. So much the better, therefore, if you don't need to use the 'Trojan horse' route. For this reason, it may be worth having a crack at using proactive methods to source invisible-market career jobs before you start on the 'Trojan horses' (for a short while at least). Thereafter, move on to twin targeting (i.e. don't stop your proactive career-job sourcing).

7.3 Applying for your first career job

The telling factor here is how you sourced the job. Answering press ads and responding to firms doing the milk rounds of colleges and universities are reactive sourcing methods where the problem is going to be competition. Cold calling, mail/faxshots, professional networks and advertising yourself in 'Employment

Wanted' columns are proactive methods, which are more hit-and-miss; but, where they hit, avoid competition. Registering with agencies is largely proactive, except that the stimulus is being provided by the agency, not you.

If you are trying to land your first career job, it is important that you use both reactive and proactive sourcing methods. In this way, and this way only, will you be able to view what the market has to offer (split into its visible and invisible constituents).

Reactive sourcing

In Chapter 3, we put great emphasis on strong points and bringing them to the fore. Strong points are your main weapon in the fight against competition, and are articulated by:

- your CV;
- your letters of application;
- what you say at interviews.

Getting strong points across is all part of the keeping-control principle – in this instance, keeping control of the messages that flow from you to the employer.

Sometimes the difficulty for newly qualified people is knowing what they have in the way of strong points. They lack any real experience, so what is there about them that they should be bringing out? Strong points only have relevance as far as a particular job is concerned. Strong points for one job won't necessarily be strong points for another. Strong points are the matches between what employers want and what you've got to offer. Clues as to what employers see as desirable attributes can be found in their advertisements and, in this case, in the kind of careers literature that some of the bigger firms put out.

Proactive sourcing

Given time and application, using proactive methods to source career jobs is intended to bring you into contact with one of the following.

- The firm with a gap in the ranks because someone from their last intake has left or had the sack. Without your proactivity, they might simply settle for being one short.
- The winter trade – the firm that shelves recruiting plans, thinking there are no college-leavers around outside the summer.
- The firm that is stimulated into recruiting by the arrival of your phone call, letter or fax.

In any of these situations, you stand a good chance of being the only applicant.

Is there anything you should look out for with proactively sourced jobs? There may be some divergence of opinion between what you and an employer see as a career job. This applies particularly to smaller firms, which may have no experience of employing anyone like you. Faced with an enthusiastic employer, being too pernickety (asking too many questions) can seem a bit like throttling the goose that's about to lay the golden egg.

What should you do in these situations? On the whole, we say run with them. Assuming you're out of work or doing fill-in jobs you can afford to take the risk of a job not turning out exactly in the way it was portrayed at the interview. Also the experience could be good if the firm is a small firm.

7.4 Applying for 'Trojan horse' jobs

'Trojan horse' jobs must meet three criteria. They must be:

- available in relative abundance;
- within your capability;
- with firms that can provide you with a career job (ultimately).

The capability test should not be too hard to satisfy, since the kind of jobs we are talking about will be jobs requiring little or nothing in the way of skills or previous experience (e.g. 'Bright young person required to . . . ').

There's no reason why 'Trojan horse' jobs shouldn't be temporary jobs (providing they're not too short-term). Including the complementary sector in your targeting will widen the choice of jobs available to you. Applying the criteria will tell you which jobs to apply for and which to leave alone.

Making your applications credible

Apart from temporary jobs (where you shouldn't be asked too many questions about your long-term plans), one of the biggest hurdles you are going to have to overcome in applying for 'Trojan horse' jobs is convincing employers that you're serious. Straight away, they will be thinking that you're acting out of desperation, or that you haven't understood the true nature of the job. They may also be harbouring the kind of doubts about overqualified people we listed on page 219.

Applying for jobs on the visible market is, as we have seen, a highly structured affair. First, you've got to get an interview, and to get an interview you need to be coming across in the right light in your CV and in your letters of application. We've already looked at your CV (by now you'll have at least two versions), so what about the letters you write in response to advertisements?

In applying for 'Trojan horse' jobs, the competition will largely come from people who are less qualified than you. The mistake, though, is to engage the competition with your qualifications, because in this instance employers may be viewing them as a drawback. Strong points, to remind you, only have relevance to a particular job and its requirements. With 'Trojan horses', strong points are more likely to be found in:

- the basic skills you have acquired;
- the experience you have had in some of your vacation jobs.

Not getting 'Trojan horse' jobs

Having done all these things, your application may still not have credibility in the eyes of some employers, and you will get turned down either with or without an interview. Your application will be stamped 'Overqualified', and that will be the end of that.

Getting turned down for career jobs is one thing, but getting turned down for jobs a 16-year-old school-leaver could do is potentially adding insult to injury. It's important here to remember that applying for 'Trojan horse' jobs is a case where you really have to keep the rejections at arm's length. Take the view that being turned down for a job because you're too good is nothing to get upset about.

Using 'Trojan horses' to access career jobs

Congratulations! You've landed a 'Trojan horse' job. You can now stop twin targeting. You won't want another 'Trojan horse', so stop your applications, because they will eat into your availability. Don't, however, stop applying for career jobs.

Once you're in a firm, you can start to use the 'Trojan horse' technique to work on the career jobs from inside. Here you've got a number of things going in your favour, notably:

- your visibility;
- firms like to promote from within (it's good for employee morale);
- if you can prove yourself, the last thing they'll want to do is lose you (not if it's avoidable).

Your first task is to excel at the job you've been recruited to do. This shouldn't be too hard, bearing in mind your abilities and the basic and routine nature of the job. Learn to bide your time, too. Don't leap out of your 'Trojan horse' in full armour on day 2, declaring your real intentions. For the trick to work, you need to dig your way into the fabric of the organisation. You will need to reach the point where the firm starts to view you as 'one of us'. Fortunately, this doesn't take as long as you might think.

During this interim period, while you are beavering away in your 'Trojan horse' job, it will pay you to try to extend your internal networks in two directions:

- upwards, at least to the level of your boss's boss;
- sideways, into the areas where the career jobs are. For instance, if you're trying to get into marketing, make sure the Marketing

Manager knows who you are. Make sure some of the people in marketing know you, too.

Being inside an organisation gives you a worm's-eye view of what's going on. For instance, you'll know if anyone in Marketing is leaving. Also, in some organisations it's policy to advertise vacancies on internal noticeboards, so make sure you keep your eye on these. As a saftey net, keep an eye on the press ads as well (just in case your firm is recruiting and it hasn't reached your ears). (You should be keeping your eye on the press ads anyway, because you're still on the market for career jobs.)

If your firm is recruiting, the signal is there for you to come out of your 'Trojan horse' immediately. Apply, and do this quickly – if possible before they start running ads or contacting employment agencies. One tip here is not to make your boss into an enemy by sidetracking him or her, or going over his or her head. Tell your boss you're going to apply for the job. In this way:

- you might enlist his or her help (a bit of string-pulling);
- you will dilute any potential hostility.

Other than a vacancy arising, how do you time your emergence from your 'Trojan horse'? Sometimes an occasion will present itself (e.g. an appraisal). Otherwise, you will have to judge when it's best – though, as a rough guide, we would say you should be aiming to reveal your true intentions after about six months: not too soon for you to be seen as a 'fly-by-night'; not too late for you to be squandering precious time.

The message you're feeding out now is a bit like the message someone fishing for promotion should be feeding out: 'I like it here, I like my work, and now I want to use my qualifications to get me into a job in . . . '. Again, speak to your boss first. Ask for his or her help and advice. With luck, this will encourage your boss to speak to other people in the organisation (i.e. to endorse you).

Do you need to put a time limit on how long you wait for the firm to come up with the goods? No, because it's not necessary.

You're still active on the career job market, remember. The time to pack your 'Trojan horse' job in is when you've got something better to go to.

Flexibility (keeping your options open)

You get a lot of first-hand experience from working in 'Trojan horse' jobs. Because of this, two unexpected things can happen to you.

- You start having a change of heart about your choice of career.
- Other career opportunities present themselves to you (ones you hadn't considered before or ones you weren't aware of). The point here is to remind you not to be over-rigid when it comes to career changes and career destinations – particularly where these choices and destinations date from a point in your past when you had far less experience of the real world. The key word is flexibility. Keep your options open and be prepared to consider anything.

Summary

In this chapter, we have considered the plight of graduates and other college-leavers who find difficulty in getting a start to their careers. The reason, in many cases, is an almost total reliance on the highly competitive visible market to provide them with what they want. Because they tend to feel that the system has cheated them ('I'm on the dole – going to university and getting a degree was a complete waste of time'), the potential for discouragement and turn-off is immense.

Very often, turn-off manifests itself in going back to college to get more qualifications. For many people, this is where the path to perpetual studentdom begins. Instead of whiling away another two years getting a master's degree in Chinese marketing, we have suggested putting your energies to better use by getting to grips with the vast, uncharted invisible market. Here we suggested two approaches.

- Proactive sourcing: cold calls, mail/faxshots, advertising yourself and professional networking.

- 'Trojan horses': applying for basic jobs with a view to worming your way into careers by attacking organisations from inside. The vast increase in the number of temporary jobs (where selection standards are minimal) has facilitated this approach.

Pursuing targets that are too narrow

A point in favour of career starters is their ability to take risks, because:

- they are mostly young, with few commitments;
- they won't be having to give anything up to take a step into the unknown.

This ability to take risks gives them the widest possible range of options, therefore it is difficult to understand why a lot of graduates and college-leavers end up pursuing targets that are far too narrow. An example of a too-narrow target is the large number of business graduates trying to get into marketing careers (nothing else will do). The reality is that marketing in the true sense of the word only tends to provide careers in fairly large firms and specialist marketing organisations. This projects a very small target (considering the number of people wanting to get in).

Getting it wrong

A difficult situation can arise when you land your first career job, then find you don't like it. What you don't know, of course, is whether you've chosen the wrong career or the wrong firm – whether you'd be perfectly happy doing the same thing somewhere else. Here are a few pointers if you find yourself in this situation.

- Take heart; it happens to a lot of people.
- Don't hand your notice in (not before you've got something else to go to). Don't, in other words, put yourself on the dole.
- Make sure you're not passing judgement on your new job prematurely. Give it a chance.
- Remember that finding another job is always easier than finding

another career, so try somewhere else first. Try ringing the changes, too – for example, if you're working in a small firm, try targeting bigger ones next time, and so on.

- Be prepared to be asked at interview why you want to leave your first job so soon. Have your answer ready. Read through our list of acceptable and unacceptable answers to the 'Why do you want to leave?' question (see page 128).
- Don't overlook the fact that you've now got some experience under your belt (however brief). Make sure this gets a mention on your CV and in your letters of application.
- If your ability to take risks can stand it, the complementary sector (temping) can provide you with the opportunity to try out the same job with different firms.

What about airing your misgivings to your boss? We would like to say yes unreservedly (if the situation can be sorted out without you having to leave, then so much the better). However, a tête-à-tête along these lines also sends out signals that you're potentially a short-term stayer, and this has risks. How you view your boss will determine whether you can have this kind of conversation or not. The last thing you want is the firm giving you the push to cut their losses on giving you training.

Questions and answers

Pay targeting: conflicting opinions on the market rate

Q *All through university, academic staff led me to believe that I would be earning around £20,000 in my first job in industry – yet three agencies I have registered with are quoting around £5,000 less than this figure. Whom should I believe?*

A The agencies (sorry to say), because they operate at the sharp end. In fairness to the staff at your university, they were probably quoting the salaries big firms pay to cream off the crop of graduates for their annual intakes.

Overqualified

Q *I am one of those people who failed to get a job when I graduated and chose to go back to university to do a master's degree. I am now back on the market again, but this time round I'm getting the distinct impression firms view me as overqualified. I am now considering leaving my master's degree off my CV, but should I be doing this?*

A The problem of overqualification tends to arise with going downmarket, and applying for the kind of jobs we've described as 'Trojan horses'. Here the answer is to ignore the turn-downs and keep going. Tampering with your CV (omitting facts to put you in a better light) is a dangerous game, so don't play it.

Putting 'Trojan horse' applications to one side, what often bothers employers about people with second and third degrees is that they fit into the image of the perpetual student – people who keep going back to college because they can't face up to the world of work. The issue, therefore, is one of motivation rather than overqualification, and you may have to treat this as one of the questions they don't ask. In other words, be ready to say something about why you went back and what you think your master's degree will bring to the job. Emphasise that going back to college was second best to getting a job.

Taking the internal route to a career – not being paid the right rate

Q *Having successfully manoeuvred myself from a clerical job into a junior management position, I received a salary increase of less than £1,000 per annum. Considering I am a graduate, and considering the responsibilities of my new position, I feel I am being exploited. Is this part of the price of being promoted internally? If so, what can I do about it?*

A What your firm has done is to view you as a clerk getting promotion rather than a graduate slotting into a graduate-type job. In other words, yes, this situation has arisen because you've come up through the ranks. What do you do about it?

Complaining isn't going to get you very far, apart from undoing some of the good work you've already done. Sadly, you're not in a very strong bargaining position yet: you need the experience more than anything and this new job, irrespective of its pay, provides you with an opportunity. Our advice would be to grin and bear it, just for now. In a little while, your value in market terms will have appreciated tremendously, and this is the time to go along to the boss and draw his attention to the fact that you're doing a management job on enhanced clerk's pay. The key is to get the boss on your side. You will best achieve this by:

- doing a good job, i.e. not letting your opinion of the pay get in the way of your performance;

- choosing your words carefully, and saying nothing which could be taken as threatening. The line to take is: 'I like it here, I want to stay here, but . . . '. If you find the boss unsympathetic, or if he or she can't do anything for you, then review your other options, including shopping the market. You've now got some experience, of course, so you will find the market far more receptive.

INDEX

accents 139, 164–5
acceptance letters 178–9
accessibility 48, 97, 158
acquiring basic skills 218
advertisements 83–6
  closing dates 99
  'Employment Wanted' columns 86
  reading job specifications 39
  and targeting cold calling 72
  for temps 201
  without salaries 91–2
  see also replying to advertisements
age 34
agencies 80-3, 184, 221
  temping for 201–2
answering machines 50, 63
application forms 103–4, 137
applying for jobs
  conveying your strong points 98, 125, 224
  delayed applications 99–100
  first career jobs 223–5
  going for wrong jobs 87–8
  halo effect 105
  interview strike rate 114
  over-reaching 36–8
  persistence 48
  re-applications 111
  rejection letters 91–2
  self-imposed limitations 39–42

  speculative applications 36–8
  targeting benchmarks 42–5, 69–70, 109–10 182
  'Trojan Horse' jobs 225–9
  unanswered applications 46–7
  see also replying to advertisements
assessment centres 118–19
attendance records 26
availability 48
  availability audit 61–2, 114
  planning holidays 61
  post-interview availability 156–7
  telephone contactability 50, 62

bad interview experiences 145–6
basic skills *see* skills
blind interviews 88, 90
borrowings 31
breaches of contract 178
broad suitability tests 140

career starting points *see* first career jobs
changes in the job market 7–10, 46
closing dates for applications 99
closing interviews 149–53
clothes 135–6
cold calling 71–3, 109, 222–3
commercial word-processing services 54–5

companies
  abdicating responsibility for careers 8
  flat organisations 21
  recruitment procedures 46–7
  researching 123–4
  small firms 7, 23–4, 35, 43
company cars 190
compensation for contractual breaches 178, 186
competition for jobs 9–10, 27, 97–8
complementary workforce 7, 200
conditional employment offers 173–4
contract work 7, 204–6
contracts of employment
  compensation for breaches of 178, 186
  restraint clauses 130–1, 163–4, 176–7
controlling events 96–7
covering letters 75, 100–2
culture clashes 174
current employment
  being persuaded to stay 181
  handing in your notice 179–81, 186
  notice periods 52, 68, 177–8
  pay buy-offs 181
  reasons for leaving 128–9
  restraint clauses 130–1, 163–4
  time off for interviews 60–1
  withdrawing your notice 186
  working your notice 184
CVs 48–60
  and application forms 103–4
  covering letters 75, 100–2
  duplicating 56
  employment history 52, 67–8
  essential information 49–53
  examination achievements 143
  faxshots 77–8
  first career jobs 219–20
  length 49, 59, 78
  mailshots 74–6
  misleading information on 68–9
  professional preparation 58–9
  recycling 57
  second opinions 56, 114
  storing 57
  two CVs 59–60, 219, 220
  typing 53–5
  updating 57–8

Daily Telegraph 85
diary planning 122–3
direct temping 202
dress 135–6
driving licences 142

e-mail shots 87
earnings *see* pay
economic conditions 7, 46
education 143
embarrassing questions 148–9
employment agencies 80–3, 184, 221
  temping for 201–2
employment experience 217
employment history 52, 67–8, 143–4
  job-hopping 20
employment offers *see* offers of employment
'Employment Wanted' columns 86
end impressions 152–3, 159
enticement 189–91
examination achievements 143
experience 217

failure at interviews 158–60
family background 142
family commitments 18–19, 29
faxing applications 102–3
faxshots 76–8, 90, 222–3
feedback 41, 113, 158–61
final interviews 117
financial planning 18–19, 29, 30–1
Financial Times 85
finding jobs 71–87
  advertisements 83–6
  approach by head-hunters 79, 90–1
  cold calling 71–3, 109
  e-mail shots 87
  employment agencies 80–3
  faxshots 76–8, 90
  Job Centres 79–80
  mailshots 74–6, 90
  networking 78–9
  recruitment consultants 80–3
  self-advertising 86
  sourcing methods
    choosing 87
    first career jobs 220–5

proactive 87, 108, 224–5
reactive 87, 108–9, 224
first career jobs
  acquiring basic skills 218
  applying for 223–9
  CVs 219–20
  market for 217
  sourcing 220–3
  Trojan Horse technique 218–19, 225–9
first impressions 56, 159
flat organisations 21
flexibility 19, 229
flexible workforce 2, 200
forced career changes 28–9
free sheets 84
freelancing 18, 206–17
  advantages 210–11
  common mistakes 209
  outsourcing 207–8
  selling yourself 209–10
  when to stop 211–12
  see also self-employment
fully flexible finances (FFF) 30–1
  see also family commitments

going to interviews 133–8
  application forms 137
  arriving late 134–5
  clothes to wear 135–6
  grooming 136–7
  items to take 133–4
  journey planning 123
  travelling expenses 137–8
golden hellos 191
graduate trainees *see* first career jobs
grievances 20–1
grooming 136–7
grudges 20–1
Guardian 85

halo effect 105
head-hunters 79, 90–1
health 142
hobbies 52, 144–5
holiday jobs 222
holidays 61, 156–7, 193
hours of work 43

interests 52, 144–5
internal promotion 232–3
interviews
  application/interview strike rate 114
  arriving late 134–5
  bad interview experiences 145–6
  blind interviews 88, 90
  closing 149–53
  clothes and grooming 135–7
  end impressions 152–3, 159
  failure at interviews 158–60
  invitations to 120–1
  items to take 133–4
  learning from 113, 158–61
  non-attendance 120
  not getting interviews 113–15
  pictures and portfolios 125–6
  planning for 122–3
  preliminary interviews 116, 138–40, 158–9
  put off by interviewers 157–8
  re-reading CVs and advertisements 122, 124–5
  rearranging 121
  researching employers 123–4
  rushed into decisions 105
  self-assessment of performance 153–4
  taking time off work for 60–1
  travelling expenses 137–8
  types of 116–19
  see also availability; questions
invisible jobs market 87

Job Centres 79–80
Job Clubs 74
job descriptions 169
job security 8, 23
job specifications 39
job titles 190
job-hopping 20
journals 85
journey planning 123

lead sheets for faxes 77
learning from interviews 113, 158–61
letters
  acceptance letters 178–9
  application letters 100–2

covering letters 75, 100–2
establishing visibility 155–6
turning jobs down 183
local newspapers 83–4
location of jobs 43
relocation packages 187–9
long service 23

mailshots 74–6, 90, 222–3
marital status 141
medical history 51
medicals 175
motivation 127
moving sideways 38
multiple targeting 95

national newspapers 84–5
negligence actions 186
networks 78–9, 222, 227–8
newspapers 83–5, 221
 see also advertisements
notice periods 52, 68, 177–8, 199
handing in your notice 179–81, 186
withdrawing your notice 186
working your notice 184

Observer 85
offers of employment 167–9
accepting
acceptance letters 178–9
handing in your notice 179–81
starting arrangements 179
avoiding bad moves 172–4
conditional offers 173–4
enticement 189–91
getting additional information 169–70
keeping yourself on the market 186–7
medicals 175
notice periods 177–8, 199
promises and prospects 190–1
references 174–5
relocation packages 187–9
responding to 168
restraint clauses 176–7
service agreements 175–6
terms and conditions 197–8
trial periods 174
turning jobs down 181–4

by letter 183
renegotiating offers 182–3
sourced through agencies 184
weighing up offers 171–2
withdrawn offers 185–6
options for people in careers 15–19
outsourcing 207–8
over-reaching 36–8
overdrafts 31
overqualified applicants 232

panel interviews 118
part-time employment 8
passed over for promotion 21–3
pay
and CV preparation 51–2
advertised and offered rates 174, 198
benchmarks 44–5, 69
and career starts 221
expectations 43, 91–2, 92–4, 115
in freelancing 211, 212
and internal promotion 232–3
pay buy-offs 181
promises of future increases 173
renegotiating offers 182–3
and swapping careers 27–8
targeting for graduate trainees 231–2
PAYE 214–15
pensions 31, 33–4, 169
perks 190
persistence 48
personal financial planning 18–19, 29, 30–1
personality clashes 25
Personnel Departments 46, 47
personnel handbooks 168–9
phones *see* telephones
photocopying services 56
pictures 125–6
portfolios 125–6
post-interview availability 156–7
preliminary interviews 116, 138–40, 158–9
preparation for interviews 122–33
diary planning 122–3
journey planning 123
pictures and portfolios 125–6

questions
  preparing answers to 126–9
  to be asked 131–3, 150
  re-reading the advertisement 124–5
  re-reading CVs 122
  researching employers 123–4
proactive sourcing methods 87, 108
  and blind interviews 88, 90
  first career jobs 224–5
  halo effect 105
  interviews from 117–18, 160
professional journals 85
professional networking 78–9, 222, 227–8
promotion prospects 21–3
psychometric tests 116
public sector 7, 25

qualifications 110–11, 219
  overqualified applicants 232
questions
  about driving licences 142
  acceptable answers 129–30
  'Are you planning to start a family?' 165–6
  'Are you subject to any restraint clauses?' 130–1, 163–4
  on education 143
  embarrassing questions 148–9
  on employment history 143–4
  on family background 142
  on health 142
  on interests/hobbies 144–5
  'Is there anything you would like to add?' 152
  on marital status 141
  points of conflict 147–8
  preparing answers to 126–9
  spotting line of questioning 146–7
  'Tell me about yourself?' 140
  to be asked 131–3, 150
  unacceptable answers 129–30
  'What do you know about us?' 126–7, 150
  on where you live 141
  'Why are you applying for this job?' 127
  'Why do you want to leave?' 128–9

re-applications 111
reactive sourcing methods 87, 108–9, 224
rearranging interviews 121
recession 7, 46
record keeping 105–6
  and cold calling 73
recruitment consultants 80-3, 111–12, 184, 221
  reference codes in advertisements 99
recruitment procedures of companies 46–7
redundancy 16, 25, 34–5, 129–30
reference codes in advertisements 99
references 53, 174–5
regional accents 139, 164–5
rejection letters 91–2
relocation packages 187–9
renegotiating offers 182–3
replying to advertisements 97–104
  application forms 103–4
  customising CVs 102
  facing up to competition 97–8
  faxing applications 102–3
  following instructions 98–100
  insufficient qualifications 110–11
  letters of application 100–2
  see also applying for jobs
researching companies 123–4
restraint clauses 130–1, 163–4, 176–7
rolling contracts 199

salaries *see* pay
second interviews 117, 150–2
self-advertising 86
self-assessment of interview performance 153–4
self-employment
  and future employment prospects 215–16
  options 208
  and tax 214–15
  and under-achieving 212
  see also freelancing
self-imposed limitations 39–42
service agreements 175–6
settlement of contracts 178
short-term employment 7

shortlists 117, 150–2, 158–60
sideways moves 38
skills 29–30, 218
  obsolescence 8, 16
  transferability 28
small firms 7, 23–4, 35, 43
smoking 64
sourcing contract work 205
sourcing first jobs 220–3
  advertising yourself 222
  agencies 221
  cold calling 222–3
  faxshots 222–3
  mailshots 222–3
  networking 222
  newspapers 221
  structuring your sourcing 223
  vacation jobs 222
sourcing jobs *see* finding jobs
speculative applications 36–8
spell-checkers 53
spotting line of questioning 146–7
starting a new job 179, 191–5
  early impressions 191–2
  first few weeks 193–5
  first morning 192–3
  late starts 192–3
staying-put 17
strategy for preliminary interviews
    139–40
structure of management jobs 21
structuring your sourcing 223
Sunday Telegraph 85
Sunday Times 85

targeting
  benchmarks 42–5, 69–70, 94, 109–10,
    182
  cold calling 72
  under-targeting 160–1
tax 214–15
technology 7, 25
telephones
  answering machines 50, 63
  answering manner 63–4
  cold calling 71–3, 109, 222–3
  contactability 50, 62
  fact-finding phone calls 169–70
temping 200–4
temporary work 7
time keeping 134–5, 192–3
toe-dipping 29
trade journals 85
training for young people 217
travelling expenses 137–8
trial periods 174
'Trojan Horse' jobs 218–20, 225–9
turning jobs down 181–4
  by letter 183
  renegotiating offers 182–3
  sourced through agencies 184
typewriters 54
typing CVs 53–5

unanswered application letters 46–7
under-targeting 160–1
unemployment 24–5, 31–2, 92–5
  multiple targeting 95
  pay expectations 92–4
  targeting benchmarks 45, 94

vacation jobs 222
visibility 154–6
  and temping 204
visionary career changes 26–8

wages *see* pay
weighing up offers 171–2
withdrawing your notice 186
withdrawn employment offers
    185–6
word-processors 53
  commercial word-processing services
    54–5
work experience 217
working your notice 184
wrong jobs 87–8